Contents

Acknowledgements

Certain sections of this book owe much to the excitement generated in the authors by Edward de Bono's writings. The book would be poorer without his influence. We would also like to acknowledge the influence of Darrell Duff's *How to Lie with Statistics* on the section on lies.

We give special thanks to James Dixey who did a great deal to initiate this project and make it possible to introduce this material to teachers all over Europe; also to Kay Hardcastle, Sam Deering, Saxon Menné, Christine Taylor and Jaime Calatayud for the valuable ideas they contributed. We would also like to thank Karl and Sophie.

Recognition is due to colleagues at schools where we tested the material, especially Marble Arch Intensive English, Pilgrims Language Courses and Davies Cambridge. Without their help and encouragement, this book would never have been finished.

Finally, we would like to thank all the students at the following schools who were the first to use this material and who offered suggestions, criticisms and support: Marble Arch Intensive English, London; Pilgrims Language Courses, Canterbury; Davies, Cambridge; Bell School, Cambridge; New School, Cambridge; Brookside School, Cambridge.

Christine Frank

Mario Rinvolucri

Marge Berer

ISBN: 9780952280880

© ELB Publishing 2008

ELB Publishing
31 George Street
Brighton
East Sussex
BN2 1RH

ELB Publishing

We are grateful to the artist Alexander Sadlo for permission to use his work "Sunset over the Sea" on the spine & to John Hooper/Hoopix Images for his skills in reproducing the original work and for the ELB Publishing logo. For more information & image library details, please visit:
www.sadloart.com

Part 1
SPEAKING

PUZZLE STORIES

Practice in asking correct questions. Ask questions about the unexplained stories and find out what they are really about.

1 A man with a pack on his back went into a field and died.

2 When the man says, 'I really don't love you', the girl will smile happily and say, 'OK, then, let's get married.'

3 The telephone rang in the middle of the night and the woman woke up. When she answered it the caller hung up. The caller felt better.

4 A black-skinned man, dressed completely in black, is walking down an unlit country road. Just as he is crossing the road, a large black car with no headlights comes rushing along. The driver manages to avoid him.

5 Two escaped prisoners went from town X to town Y. The people following them were sure they had gone from town Y to town X.

6 Two men look up round a corner and see something that makes them want to go down.

7 These two girls can see very well in the dark. All day they lie in a corner of the kitchen.

8 A man walked into a bar in Texas. He asked for a glass of water. The barman pointed his gun at him. The man said, 'Thank you' and walked out.

9 There was a small hut in the desert. It was empty except for a dead man hanging by a rope from the roof. Outside stood a lorry.

10 A girl lies heart-broken on the floor. Beside her is a piece of wood. There is sawdust in the rubbish bin.

11 A man went from town A to town B by train. On the way the train went through a tunnel. In town B the man went to see a person. After the meeting he was very happy. He took the train back to A. When the train went into the tunnel he threw himself from the train.

12 A couple lie dead in a room. A dog is trying to get out of the room.

13 These twins don't live at home. They are always having terrible nightmares about a kitchen and a dining-room.

14 A man heard a sound and swam towards it. He was drowned.

15 Two men will be having a boxing match. One man will be quite unable to knock the other one down.

16 A woman committed a crime. The police arrested her and took her to court. The judge didn't know what to do about her.

17 A couple will build a square house. In each wall they'll have a window and each window will face north.

18 All the men from the village were drowned because their boats were stranded.

19 A man had his arms out through the sides of a telephone booth. The phone was off the hook. Outside the booth was a black bag on the ground.

20 A person passed a window. A phone rang. The person screamed.

THREE-ITEM STORIES

Practice in asking correct questions. Ask questions and find out what the story is which links the three items.

1 Accident/wreckage/no dead or injured

2 Fire/glass/ship

3

4 Pianist/concert/panic

5 Punishment/fence/friends

6

7 Bus-driver/wedding/birth

8 Siege/starvation/ox

9

 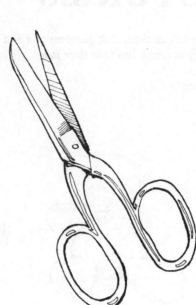 

10 Smuggling/shoes/cloudburst

11 Crime/paintings/satisfied victim

12

SWITCH SENTENCES

Short intensive discussion. Explain and discuss the meaning of the statements. Then switch the statements around and discuss them again.

1 The women formed the club.

   a Coffee, knitting and gossip.
   b Y.W.C.A.
   c Entertainment for middle-class housewives.
   d Voluntary work – who is helped?
   e 'And the women come and go
       Talking of Michelangelo.' (T. S. Eliot)
   f Leaders emerge.
   g Personalities clash.

   Television created idleness.
   Money doesn't mean happiness.
   The newspapers influence public opinion.

2 Schools are like prisons.

   a Education for life.
   b Work without pay.
   c Preparation to live in society.
   d Rehabilitation.
   e Are they there too long?
   f Why a uniform?
   g They don't learn enough.
   h Why do they come back?

   Government invades privacy.
   The entertainer delighted the audience.
   Children need their parents.

3 People cause accidents.

   a One-parent families.
   b Death toll on the roads alarming.
   c Most accidents happen in the home.
   d The housewife is accident-prone.
   e Contraceptive methods don't always work.
   f Keep medicines out of reach of children.
   g Prevention is better than cure.
   h When you drink, don't drive.

   Freedom means responsibility.
   Rich men help their country.
   Houses are homes.

4 All children become adults.

   a Why do we need more old peoples' homes?
   b Give them something to learn and do.
   c They need toys.
   d They need attention and care.
   e The family rejects them.
   f They get new teeth.
   g She doesn't know how old she is.
   h The older she gets the sillier she becomes.

   People shape the environment.
   Talking isn't always communication.
   People control machines.

5 Industry determines the landscape.

   a Skyscrapers on the Spanish coast.
   b Atomic reactors being built in Britain.
   c Forests and rivers dead.
   d Antarctica.
   e Nuclear waste a major problem.
   f The motorway system expands.
   g Why is London a city of over ten million?
   h The surface of the Moon.

   Women have the same potential as men.
   Criminals are the reason for prisons.
   Fashion influences people.

6 To live to eat.

   a Overweight is not healthy.
   b His trousers don't fit any more.
   c Butter mountain.
   d To be slim is modern.
   e Thousands die of heart disease.
   f Thousands die of malnutrition.
   g Enough for our need, not for our greed.
   h More education on nutrition is required.

   All students are intelligent people.
   Politicians are in the hands of the people.
   Without workers there would be no strikes.

7 When wages rise they inflate prices.

   a A fair day's pay for a fair day's work.
   b Greed.
   c The pursuit of profits.
   d The oil crisis.
   e The decline in living standards.
   f Do prices *ever* come down?
   g Falling behind and catching up.
   h Price control and wage restraint.

   Programmed learning makes programmed
   people.
   Gravediggers presuppose corpses.
   Marriage prepares you for divorce.

8 Unemployment causes poverty.

   a Living on the dole.
   b The destruction of communities.
   c The Third World.
   d Emigration.
   e Industrial deserts.
   f Education and training costs money.
   g Unearned income.
   h I'd be lost without a job to go to.

   Action is no good without reflection.
   Being tired makes people emotional.
   Prostitutes degrade society.

9 Animals are our friends.

   a Guide dogs for the blind.
   b Keeping up with the Joneses.
   c R.S.P.C.A.
   d I'd be happiest on a desert island.
   e Wanted: good home for a kitten.
   f With friends like that, who needs enemies?
   g Everyone except me is overweight.
   h Why kill to eat?

   The more we learn, the less we know.
   The truth destroyed the myth.
   Foreigners are nasty people.

SWITCH PHOTOS

Short intensive discussion. Explain and discuss the relationship between the two photographs. Then switch them around and discuss them again.

1

2

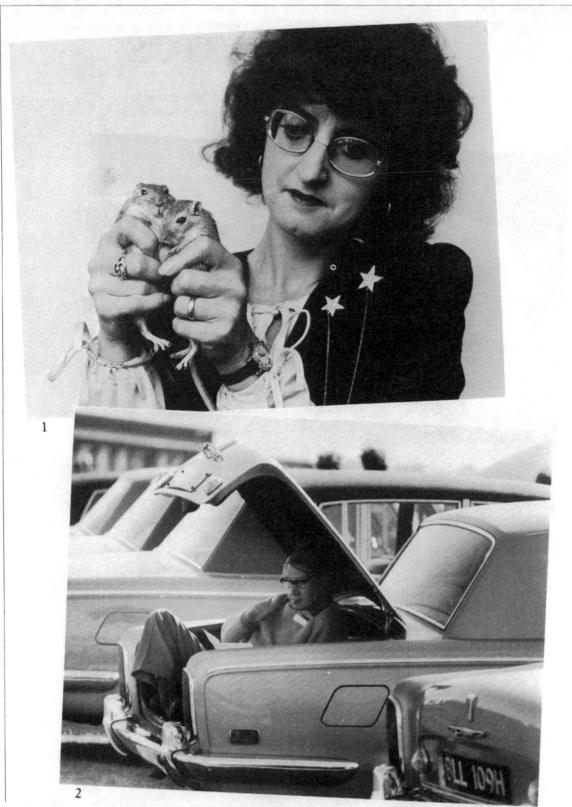

1

2

1

2

1

2

1

2

CAUSES AND CONSEQUENCES

Intensive discussion. Discuss all the possible causes and consequences of these factual statements.

1 Traffic accidents have increased 20% in West Germany this year.
Doctors in rich countries advise people to stay slim.
The middle classes are learning more English.

2 The birth rate has declined considerably in Britain in the last ten years.
There are many graduates among the unemployed.
Churches attract old people.

3 Alcoholism amongst women is increasing.
Europeans have a high life expectancy.
More men are wearing wigs.

4 Divorce is on the increase.
The world is divided into two power blocks.
Television has replaced reading for many children.

5 Illiteracy is a serious problem among adults.
Inflation continues.
The Open University in Britain attracts middle-class housewives.

6 Many Europeans are emigrating to Australia.
Old people in Northern Europe are often lonely.

Foreign workers in a country are often unhappy.

7 More people are becoming interested in solar energy.
Scandinavian countries have high suicide rates.
Natural fibres are replacing synthetics in the clothing industry.

8 Pollution makes people angry.
Grazing animals enlarge deserts.
A *coup d'état* is a usual way of changing a government.

DESIGNS

Discussion and criticism of the designs of everyday objects.

The bath

A Ask and answer these questions in pairs or groups.

1 Do you prefer to have a bath or a shower? Why?
2 How long do you spend in the bath or shower?
3 What's wrong with the way baths are designed?

4 What do you do in a sauna bath?
5 Do you bath alone in your country, or with other people?
6 Did the Romans bath alone? Do the Japanese? Do children?

B Now have a look at this ultra-modern bath.

a A soft pillow.
b An inter-com microphone to talk to people in other rooms.
c A towel you can pull down if you get water in your eyes.
d A reading lamp.
e A book on a lectern that lowers from the ceiling.

f A button which opens the bathroom door when you press it.
g A button to turn off the inter-com system.
h A hot and cold water mixing control.
i An extension phone.
j Two pipes bringing water silently into the bath.
k Two large diameter pipes to drain the bath fast.

C Answer these questions in pairs or groups.

1 What kind of person is this bath for?
2 What do you like about this bath?

3 What's wrong with it?
4 How could it be improved?

D Now you design *your* ideal bath.

The traffic jam car

A Ask and answer these questions in pairs.

1 Have you ever got stuck in a traffic jam?
   When? Where? How long for?
2 Were you in a hurry?
3 How did you and the other people in the car
   feel?
4 What did you do to pass the time?
5 What did the people in the cars around you
   do?
6 Are cars properly designed for stopping and
   starting in traffic jams?

B Now have a look at this traffic jam car.

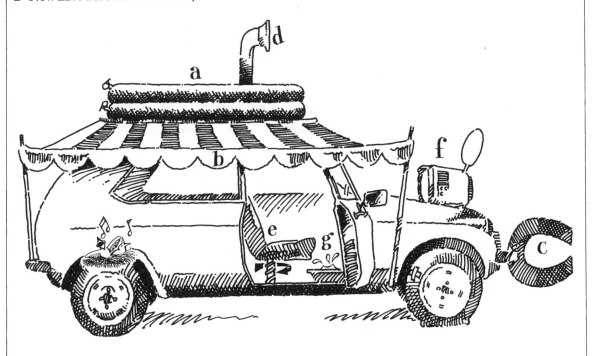

a Roof swimming-pool for children.
b Awning to keep the sun off.
c Magnet on front bumper to grip rear bumper
   of next car in queue.
d Periscope to see over the cars in front and
   behind.
e Reversible seat so you can change the view.
f Video TV.
g Cool foot-bath.

C Ask and answer these questions in pairs.

1 What kind of person would want a car like
   this? An impatient person? A sociable one?
   A commercial traveller?
2 What do you like about this car?
3 What's wrong with it?
4 How could it be improved?

D Now you design *your* ideal traffic jam car.

The TV phone

A Make a list of the sorts of phone conversations you usually have.

1 In which of these would you like to see the other person?

2 In which of these would you like to be seen by them?

B Suppose you had a 'vision on/vision off' switch so that the other person could see you or not. In the following situations would you want to be seen? Why?

1 You are lying about why you can't go to their boring party.

2 You are asking your bank manager for an overdraft.

3 You are ringing your parents long distance.

4 You are proposing to your boy/girl friend.

5 You are ringing the police station to report something suspicious happening outside your house.

C If you had a TV phone, where would you put it in your house and why?

1 Kitchen?
2 Bedroom?
3 Living-room?

4 Hall?
5 Dining-room?
6 Or would you want a portable unit?

D To which of the following people would a TV phone be useful in their jobs and in what way?

1 Photographer
2 Butcher
3 University teacher
4 Salesperson

5 Sheep farmer
6 Estate agent
7 Housewife

E Now design a TV phone you could put in your house or flat. You should include:

a incoming picture screen
b monitor screen (so you can see the picture of you that's going out)
c appropriate lighting

d picture and sound control panel
e background furniture and decoration
f microphones and/or loudspeakers

No stairs

A Ask and answer these questions in pairs.

1 Are stairs a good way of changing floors?

2 Who finds stairs difficult, dangerous or impossible to use?

3 What are some of the advantages and disadvantages of living on two floors or more?

4 Why doesn't everyone live on one floor?

B Ramps, lifts, and escalators are some of the devices that make stairs unnecessary. What would the advantages or disadvantages of each of these be in a house?

C Design a new way to get from the ground floor to the first floor of a house.

Change this classroom

Look around the room you are in.

A Is this room good as a classroom? Why? Why not?

B Could this room be used as a bedroom? A nightclub? A doctor's surgery?

C Suggest other ways this room could be used.

D Choose one of your suggestions and re-design this room. Put everything in it you would need.

Change this building

Get a picture in your mind of the building you are in.

A Is this building a good one for a school?

B Could this building be used as a hotel? A zoo? A hospital? A palace?

C Suggest other ways this building could be used.

D Choose one of your suggestions and re-design this building. Draw and list everything you would need to put in it.

CONTEXT AND MEANING

The meaning of a very simple statement depends on who says it, who they are speaking to and where the two people are. Because the people are both in the situation, the meaning is clear to them – it doesn't need to be said. For example:

STATEMENT	MEANING	CONTEXT
'The door is open.'	You forgot to lock it again, idiot!	A bank manager to a clerk standing in front of the safe first thing in the morning.
	What a relief! Now I don't have to sit out here waiting for someone to come home.	A person arrives home without a key, no one is there, the person tries the door and it opens.
	No wonder I'm cold.	A person sitting in a draughty room that is freezing cold.
	Shut the door.	Two people in an office. It's very noisy next door but the speaker doesn't want to get up.
	Please come in.	A receptionist in an office; someone has just rung the bell or knocked.

In each of the following exercises, you are given:

a a statement and the context it was said in – you say what it means.
b a statement and what it means – you supply the context.
c a statement – you think of all the meanings and contexts.

Exercise 1

STATEMENT	MEANING	CONTEXT
a 'It's raining.'		Mother to young son dressed only in T-shirt and shorts who is going outside.
		Farmer to harvesters.
		Noah to his wife.
		Man dying of thirst at sea in a small boat.
		Driver with broken wipers to passenger in car on dark road.

STATEMENT	MEANING	CONTEXT
b 'I feel tired.'	I don't want to make love. It's time you went home. Carry me. I'm ready to die. I've done enough work today.	
c 'He's not answering.'		

Exercise 2

STATEMENT	MEANING	CONTEXT
a 'The sun's coming up.'		Two spies are bugging an embassy office. The alarm clock didn't go off and they wanted to catch a dawn train. Two climbers are stranded on a mountain ledge. Woman to man. (One of them is married.) Search party camped in a wood where they are looking for a lost child. Farmer to his wife in bed sleeping.
b 'I do wish they'd get here.'	The dinner's getting burnt and I'm hungry. I hope there hasn't been an accident. I can't wait any longer – I should have left ages ago. It's been years; I'm dying to see them. I want to get this over with as soon as possible.	
c 'I've got a headache.'		

Exercise 3

STATEMENT	MEANING	CONTEXT
a 'I've had this dress for years.'		Wife to husband showing him an old worn-out dress.
		Girl to boyfriend. She's afraid he doesn't think she looks nice.
		Woman talking to friend about gaining and losing weight.
		Woman explaining to charity shop why she's giving them a perfectly good dress.
		Two women talking about fashion.
b 'Want a cigarette?'	Notice me.	
	Shall we have a break?	
	I dare you to smoke.	
	Have you really stopped smoking?	
	I want one of your cigarettes afterwards.	
c 'Would you like to stay the night?'		

Exercise 4

STATEMENT	MEANING	CONTEXT
a 'I don't know what to say.'		Woman opens birthday present from man – it's an engagement ring.
		Person receives cheap gaudy gift as wedding present from family friend who is waiting for reaction.
		Very honest person to friend who wants help stealing some money.
		Person who has recently received two pay rises asks for a third. Boss reacts.

STATEMENT	MEANING	CONTEXT
b 'When are you coming back?'	Please ask me to go with you.	
	Are you coming back at all?	
	I need to know – someone might phone.	
	Don't you dare be late!	
	Where are you really going?	
	Do you have to go?	
	I'm afraid of being alone.	
c 'No need to explain.'		

Exercise 5

STATEMENT	MEANING	CONTEXT
a 'I think I'd better get down to work.'		Two people in a library. One is chatting on endlessly, the other wants to work.
		Two people having coffee and a very interesting conversation.
		A journalist with a dead-line in an hour and she hasn't even begun the article.
		Person who's in danger of losing their job.
		Husband to wife after big dinner party looking at piles of dirty dishes.
b 'Well, what do you think?'	I think it's awful but don't want to say so.	
	You know better than me in these things.	
	I haven't thought about it at all.	
	I dare you to say you don't like it.	
	Don't just sit there – say something!	
c 'It's a little late for that.'		

Exercise 6

STATEMENT	MEANING	CONTEXT
a 'Where do you think you're going?'		Foreman to worker who is leaving before the shift ends.
		Father to 15-year-old son who says he's going to a strip club.
		Flat mate to girl getting ready to go to a formal party – she is putting on an old shirt and jeans.
		Person carrying lots of packages bumps into rude man.
b 'His glass is half empty.'	Pour him another drink.	
	Now he's sure to die.	
	Let's hope he buys us another.	
	Maybe he *does* like the taste of it.	
	Oh no! He's been drinking again!	
c 'He needs a change.'		

Exercise 7

STATEMENT	MEANING	CONTEXT
a 'No, I'm not hungry, thank you.'		Person in a filthy restaurant to waitress waiting to take her order.
		Guest at a dinner party who has already had four helpings.
		Hungry hitchhiker to driver. Driver has already gone out of his way to help hitchhiker.
		It's her turn to pay. He's just ordered a very expensive dinner, she's short of money.
b 'I'll get in touch with you next week.'	Don't call. I don't want to see you.	
	There's nothing to worry about.	
	I'll know for sure by then.	
	I won't have any time till then.	
	I'd like to see you some time, but I don't know when.	
c 'I love you.'		

Part 2
READING AND SPEAKING

TWO-IN-ONE STORIES

Intensive reading. Sort out the two stories as quickly as you can. Then re-tell them.

The stork

The company chairman

1 The cook stole a leg from a beautiful roast stork just before it was served to the king.

2 'But, your Majesty, you didn't clap last night.'

3 He glowered at them. 'Gentlemen, I have something I must say: half of you are idiots.'

4 The king asked him angrily why the bird had only one leg.

5 One day a company chairman got very angry with his board of directors.

6 The king clapped his hands and the birds flew off. 'There,' he said, 'You see, they all have two legs the moment I clap.'

7 'Very well,' the chairman said, 'I withdraw it – half of you are *not* idiots.'

8 Next morning the cook and the king went down to the river and saw the storks all standing on one leg.

9 One of the directors stood up and banged on the table. 'I demand that you withdraw that last observation, Mr Chairman.'

10 The cook replied, 'Storks only ever have one leg – come to the river with me tomorrow and I will show you, Your Majesty.'

The farmer
The invitation

1 'Well,' said the farmer, scratching his chin, 'I'll tell you what we do.'

2 'Why do I have to use my elbow and my foot?' asked his friend.

3 A man inviting his friend to his home explained to him where he lived.

4 The man went back to his car with a puzzled look on his face and said to his wife, 'I think he must be crazy.'

5 'Come to the third floor,' he said, 'and where you see the letter E on the door, push the button with your elbow and when the door opens put your foot against it.'

6 'We eat what we can and what we can't eat we can.'

7 A curious tourist, after passing a huge field of carrots alongside the road, stopped and asked the farmer what he did with his large crop.

8 'He said they ate what they could and what they couldn't they could.'

9 'Well,' exclaimed the man, 'You're not going to come empty-handed, are you?'

A stranger in London
The new hedge clipper

1 The stranger got out and ran up to a policeman.

2 He was about half way round his garden when his neighbour arrived.

3 Then he disappeared into Waterloo station.

4 'Thanks very much,' was the grateful reply.

5 'Would you mind paying my fare, officer?' he said. 'I've a train to catch.'

6 He called a taxi and asked the driver to take him to Waterloo, mentioning that he had a train to catch at three o'clock.

7 'That's all right, at least I can now go back to bed and sleep in peace,' he said, walking back to his own house.

8 One Saturday morning a friend of mine decided to use his new hedge clipper.

9 The policeman told him and the stranger handed him the money.

10 The job was quickly finished and my friend thanked his neighbour for his help.

11 'Can I give you a hand?' the neighbour asked my friend.

12 At half past two the taxi drew up at Waterloo, the driver smiling broadly.

13 'What is the fare from Euston to Waterloo?' he asked the policeman.

14 A stranger arrived at Euston just before midday.

15 For two hours he sat back enjoying the sights of London.

The railway ticket

Aesop's fable

1 There were eight of us in the carriage, and seven tickets were soon found and punched.

2 A few hours later a mean-looking traveller came down the road, and he too stopped and asked Aesop, 'Tell me, my friend, what are the people of Athens like?'

3 Aesop, the Greek writer of fables, was sitting by the road one day when a friendly traveller asked him, 'What sort of people live in Athens?'

4 'All tickets, please!' said the railway inspector, appearing at the door of the carriage.

5 Frowning, the man replied, 'I'm from Argos and there the people are unfriendly, mean, deceitful and vicious. They're thieves and murderers, all of them.'

6 'Funny thing, absence of mind,' said the helpful traveller when the inspector had gone. 'Absence of mind?' said the old man.

7 But the old man in the corner went on searching through his pockets, looking very unhappy.

8 Aesop replied, 'Tell me where you come from and what sort of people live there, and I'll tell you what sort of people you'll find in Athens.'

9 So he was, and the inspector looked anything but pleased as he hastily punched the mangled ticket.

10 Smiling, the man answered, 'I come from Argos, and the people there are all friendly, generous and warm-hearted. I love them all.'

11 Again Aesop replied, 'Tell me where you come from and what people are like there and I will tell you what the people are like in Athens.'

12 'I was chewing off last week's date!'

13 'You haven't lost your ticket,' said the man next to him, helpfully. 'You're holding it in your teeth!'

14 At this Aesop answered, 'I'm happy to tell you, my dear friend, that you'll find the people of Athens much the same.'

15 'I'm afraid you'll find the people of Athens much the same,' was Aesop's reply.

The loan
The burglar

1 'That's not so hard, George,' said his father. 'Write to him and say you need the £1000 at once.'

2 Among my best friends are Joe and his wife Alice, who live in a nice little house near Manchester.

3 'You mean the £500,' George interrupted.

4 The friend proved to be untrustworthy, and as George thought he would lose the £500, he asked his father for advice.

5 The donor neglected to send his name, and all day the couple's question was, 'Wonder who it is?'

6 'No, I don't! Say a thousand pounds and he will write back he only owes you £500.'

7 There was a note from the burglar propped up on the pillow in the bedroom saying, 'Now you know.'

8 When, as a newly married couple, they had just returned from their honeymoon, they got a pleasant surprise in the post one morning – two tickets to the best show in town.

9 George Smith had lent a friend £500 but he had nothing in writing confirming the loan.

10 They enjoyed the show; when they reached home they found that their house had been broken into and that all their wedding presents had been taken.

11 'Then you'll have it in writing.'

The general's visit

No teeth

1 He immediately ordered a pool and courts to be built.

2 Some weeks later Peter met his friend in the street, and the friend asked him what had happened.

3 Peter had been called up, but he didn't want to join the army, so he asked his friend what he should do.

4 When he was asked why he would not give benches to primary children but wanted prisoners to have a swimming pool, he replied, 'Do you think I will ever go back to primary school?'

5 His friend said, 'Well, why don't you have all your teeth pulled out? You won't get past the medical then.'

6 A general visited a primary school where the children said they had no benches to sit on.

7 Some time later he visited a prison. The men there complained they had no swimming pool and no tennis courts.

8 Peter, who had no teeth left, mumbled, 'The officer said I was no good to the army – I've got flat feet!'

9 He told the kids there *were* no benches – they must make sacrifices for their country.

CONTRADICTIONS

Intensive reading. Read one sentence of the stories at a time, and then comment on what you have read.

1 John Brown is a butcher who always sells good stale bread. One morning last week as he was busy working in his office a lady came in and ordered six loaves and four apples. John had never had such a large order before and he suggested bringing the cakes and sandwiches to her house in his van. So at 10 a.m. after a hard day's work John put on his overcoat and scarf and stepped out into the sunny June evening. As he approached his customer's tent John took the goods from the basket of his bicycle and walked up the front path to hand over the vegetables to the lady waiting in the reception hall.

2 My neighbour John has just called in to say that he and his wife can come to my party next Wednesday. So we've arranged to meet outside the cinema at about six o'clock. The main film showing is the latest James Bond film, starring Sophia Loren, Henry Kissinger and Clark Gable. After the service the two of us will probably go for a drink. It's a long time since I saw John and his wife, so I'm looking forward to an enjoyable Saturday evening with them.

3 John Adams is an amateur detective who spends all his time trying to solve crimes. Yesterday at about nine o'clock in the afternoon he saw his brother Joe walk up to a red car, get into it and ride off at a steady trot. Three days later at exactly the same time he thought he saw the same thing. He couldn't be absolutely sure as it was already getting dark and the woman was holding an umbrella over her face to protect her from the fog. Later that day when Adams had observed several other suspicious people he walked to the next village and handed his report to the head waiter at New Scotland Yard.

4 Smith Billy is a teacher at a riding school. He always gets up at five to prepare his lessons in order to avoid waking his children by his singing. He takes his noiseless typewriter and writes four or five pages of notes so he will not hesitate when he lectures to his horses. For variety, when his lessons are in danger of becoming too interesting, he sometimes copies out a science fiction story from Grimm or Hans Anderson, which he can dictate to the horses. Occasionally there is an emotional reaction from his docile donkeys: when the story is sad they laugh. Billy prefers this job to the one he had in a language school because now his students never take him for a ride.

5

San Antonio

How about a holiday in San Antonio, the newest resort on the Costa Brighton? The beaches with sand as soft as concrete, skating in the warm sea and running through the pine forests have been popular with our regular visitors for over 400 years. The cafés, hospitals and hoverports offer real Russian dancing, authentic flamenco and fandango accompanied by throbbing chess-playing and singing to fill your mind with memories to be treasured for minutes.

6 If you want a new car for the family then come along to our surgery and look at our latest discoveries. We have imported cars as well as a wide range produced in British kitchens. There are no vehicles here on display so just come along any time to see them.

Alternatively you could phone and we'd be delighted to give you our catalogues personally. We are open from 3 a.m. – 7 a.m., seven days a year and are looking forward to buying from you the car you've been dreaming of.

7   My friend Peter, who is 23 years old and a bachelor, has just bought a 14th century bungalow on the estate behind our house. I have known Peter ever since we started school together 32 years ago, and was delighted to hear he would be living so near. Last Sunday we decided to visit him and his wife in their new home and we got the bus at the Town Hall. It took us about 35 minutes to get there, although I have to admit we didn't walk very fast. Peter and his eldest daughter, who had just returned home from work, were looking out for us through the letterbox and waved as they saw us arrive. We parked the car at the bus stop, put 75p in the parking meter and ran up the path and in through the window. Peter's wife was upstairs making tea and she told us that her husband would be home in about half an hour.

8   Joan lives alone in a large house near the city centre. Every evening she gets up, wakes her family and gets ready to go to work in the town twelve miles away. She takes her bike out of the stable and rides off into the warm December morning. As she passes the gardens in front of the rows of shops she notices the roses that are just coming into bloom. When she stops at the traffic lights she takes out her thermometer. She sees it's three o'clock and thinks of her mother who will be waiting at home for her to return from school. At last the traffic lights turn blue and she drives off along the footpath to her two-room flat.

9   Three years ago I retired from work and have since spent the whole time travelling. As I didn't get very much pension my parents gave me £100 for my 21st birthday. I took the cross-channel ferry from Birmingham to Moscow and made my way through Spain to Copenhagen. The gift from my parents together with the £560 a week pension made it possible for me to stay in cheap guest houses all the time. In Denmark I met my grandson and we spent two days together travelling by boat to Rome. After two nights at the Hilton Hotel we returned home by taxi. It was a wonderful journey and a year that I'll never forget.

10 *14 Eaton Terrace*
An inferior house with full gas-fired central freezing. It is situated in one of the worst residential areas of the city close to the local rickshaw service and within flying distance of the airport. The property, which is poorly built of cardboard under a glass roof, was completed by a local baker about eight years ago and is in immaculate order throughout. It is regarded as a historical monument although in need of repair.

11 I have lived in the centre of London for the last ten years and will be moving to a cottage in a small village next month. When I moved in I was only two years old so I enjoyed the large garden and fields that surrounded our farm. When I went to school it became more difficult, as I had to take the underground to the nearest airport and from there went by tractor. Anyway all that is over now and I am looking forward to the nice little penthouse flat that will soon be my home.

MATCHINGS

Fast reading. In pairs or groups, discuss what the headlines mean.
Then match the headline to the corresponding article.

THE SUN ON YOUR FACE WITHOUT THE WIND IN YOUR HAIR.

1

HOW THE WAGE CONTROLS HIT ONE FAMILY

I _____ – easy ground for rapists.

3

"My son-in-law sent me!"

4

2

'GOODNIGHT' WITH HIGH HOPES

5

The Socially Seductive Kiss with the promise of fun times ahead. For the very special guest . . . from the host with something extra special in mind. Goodnight, and next time . . .

a

In I _____ six youths were cleared of a rape charge. The judge believed the woman was 'willing', (even though she was covered with bruises when found by a passer-by minutes after the rape), because she had been drinking and knew some of the youths. She was an itinerant woman.

b

I have to make most of the kids' clothes or else they would have to go round in rags. Just now they all need new shoes for the winter and they're having to wear their summer sandals.

'There's often nothing left in my purse at all by Tuesday and Steve doesn't get paid till Thursday

c

TAXIDERMIST

d

Until now, BMW have had but two objections to the joys of open air motoring.

The first was that once the vehicle exceeded walking pace an internal air flow was created that made woolly hats and head scarves compulsory.

The second was that the vagaries of the weather, particularly in Britain, only offered you a handful of summer days on which you could relish such pleasures.

The new BMW Cabriolet now provides the solution to both these problems.

e

Fascist Attacks Continue

1

Why psychiatrist poured white paint over the black Granada

2

'Angel' snatched by mum

3

SUPERINTENDENT

(Salary £9,457 to £10,777 p.a. incl. if qualified)

4

"If there were dreams to sell what would you buy?"

5

I don't know where to go, or who to go to

6

Your Rights

7

Why don't they

8

Sagging spaghetti

9

HEALTH OFFICIALS TO TELL INTERESTS

10

The department of transport moved smartly this week to try to nip a budding row over its handling of the repairs to the crumbling motorway-on-stilts in the Midlands. Parliamentary under-secretary Mr Kenneth Clarke, transport spokesman on the faults discovered last October that have threatened 13 miles of viaduct around Spaghetti Junction in Birmingham, started publishing a weekly account of work being undertaken and its effect on motorists using the M5/M6 motorways.

a

... invent a really smart waterproof rain hat? Scarves and hats go soggy, umbrellas can be a nuisance and those plastic hoods look dreadful. Some sort of headgear that's both trendy and efficient is long overdue.—June Haigh-Jones, Shrewsbury, Shropshire.

b

A psychiatrist claimed he was defending his property when he poured paint over a car parked outside his home in Bayswater.

He splashed the white gloss paint on Mr. Michael Hart's car — a black Granada.

c

Leigh Road is the third of our provision for Mentally Handicapped Children and with our other units will provide flexibly for long-term, short-term and respite care.

The Superintendent will assit in the commissioning of the unit, selecting potential residents, whilst developing the Borough's policy of Social Care.

Applicants should be experienced in the care of children with developmental handicaps and should be qualified in Social Work or a related discipline.

d

SOMETIME during the night of June 24/25 New Beacon Bookshop – of 76 Stroud Green Road, Finsbury Park, London N.4. – was vandalised with the slogan 'Blacks Out' scrawled across the brickwork below the shop glass window.

e

FLYAWAY tug-of-love girl Nicola Darnborough was with her mother in South Africa last night.

The news came after Nicola's father pleaded to his ex-wife: " Please return my little angel."

f

Health officials are to follow in the footsteps of local councillors by declaring their outside interests.

This move suggested by a Royal Commission inquiry, is aimed at preventing another Poulson - type bribes scandal.

g

In the chilly depths of next winter, just when most people are wrapping up warm to ward off colds, a few fortunate people will sail away on Queen Elizabeth 2 to all those magical-sounding places on the other side of the globe.

h

I'm 19 and live with my family. For the past seven years I've been deeply depressed. I attempted suicide once and ended up in hospital. I've been to a psychiatrist once, called on the social services and rung up the Samaritans. Friends have given valuable time to me. But all this help gets me nowhere.

i

Confusion about the shop's legal obligation to the customer always gets worse at sale time. Despite the fact that the majority of shops display enormous disclaimer 'No Refunds On Sale Goods' notices you do have exactly the same rights when you buy during a sale as at any other time.

j

WHALES HAVE BRAINS MORE COMPLEX THAN ANY SPECIES, INCLUDING MAN

1

Jury disqualify Bay Bea: Britain go into lead

2

Pack up and go!

3

New bid to end hunger strikes

4

missing LINKS?

5

" What's this, overtime? "

6

NOW U.S. DOCTORS SLAM CIVIL DEFENCE

7

The slim blue line

9

SMALL TALK

8

France rushes industry takeover

10

If half as much energy and enthusiasm were channelled into planning a holiday wardrobe as in planning the holiday itself much confusion would be happily avoided.

Packing puts even the most orderly of organisers into a panic. Each summer our fashion department is flooded with pleas for what to pack for readers who are accompanying their husbands on business trips to Europe, taking coach journeys through the Alps or sabbaticals to the Far East, and for the lucky few, planning far away cruises to the tropics.

a

b

BRITAIN, who finished joint second behind the United States in yesterday's third inshore race of the international series at Cowes, took the team lead in the Admiral's Cup last night after the International Jury disqualified the American yacht Bay Bea.

c

THE FRENCH government has overruled its own doubters and decided to act swiftly to nationalise industries as planned in President Mitterrand's election programme — amounting to one fifth of French industry.

A three-stage programme to be unveiled in the National Assembly today by the Prime Minister, Mr Mauroy, is expected to announce the takeover of banks (including extensive industrial holdings held by banks), armaments, and steel in the autumn.

f

THE Government decided last night to send in a representative to the Maze Prison in an attempt to end the IRA hunger strike.

An official from the Northern Ireland office is expected to read out to the prisoners a statement outlining terms for a solution.

d

They used to be the essential small accessory for the big businessman. But in the past few years, the price of pocket tape recorders has come down – and you're now as likely to find one in a handbag or a trouser pocket as in the hand of a captain of industry. They are emerging from the business machine world to be used for shopping lists, interviews, telephone conversations – and even for listening to music.

e

MORE young policewomen are joining the fight against crime as growing numbers of men quit the force.

And if present recruitment trends continue eventually there could be more women officers than men, police chiefs were told yesterday.

g

THEY HAVE BEEN HUNTED TO THE BRINK OF EXTINCTION TO MAKE MINK FOOD, MARGARINE, COSMETICS, FERTILIZER, WHALE STEAKS AND LUBRICATING OIL.

There are cheap, plentiful substitutes for all whale products. But the massacre of the whales continues, led by Norway, Iceland, Spain, the Soviet Union and Japan. This year, more than 15,000 of these highly-intelligent marine mammals will suffer agonizing deaths as they are chased down at sea and blasted with massive harpoons.

i

MEET PEOPLE IN LONDON
with whom you have something in common.
LINKUP offers a fresh approach to making friends in London by linking you with on going groups of members who share your interests.

LINKUP groups go out together in town and locally for meals/drinks/films/theatre/music/walks/swimming/Sunday brunches/parties/etc, escape to the country or just meet at someone's place for a coffee. Each group is different, of course, but the atmosphere is always informal and friendly.

h

"If the civil defence budget were in my hands, I would spend all $120 million on morphine," says one American scientist who has studied the effects of nuclear war. "Civil defence money is worse than wasted now. It misleads. It may let people believe they can get away in a nuclear war. They can't."

j

ROD'S SECRET LOVE

1

The Midland explores some alternatives to opening a bank account.

Corsican 2
guerrilla chief
surrenders

WHAT PRICE PROGRESS?

3   4

We've Had Enough

Scientists
establish

5
firmer tests

"He Didn't Give Us Anything"

of paternity

6

Why Pick on us?

8

7

9

Simon's sunk galleon proves experts wrong

10

The days of the housewife in the Twenties and Thirties, with very few labour saving devices, are so often talked about as the "Hard Days". Maybe they were in some respects: cars were a luxury for the few, there were no hypermarkets, supermarkets or shopping precincts, yet they had many advantages over the modern ways of life. In spite of our sophisticated ways of modern shopping, in those "Hard Days", it was a more relaxed and pleasurable experience.

a

It was the toughest audience the Great Communicator had faced since taking the oath of office. At most, 10% of the nation's black voters cast ballots for Ronald Reagan last year, and the President has done nothing since then to gain their confidence. Of the 450 top jobs in his Administration, only about 15 have gone to blacks, and his budget cuts will most immediately and severely affect the nation's poor, who are disproportionately black.

d

SCHOOLBOY diver Simon Burton was convinced he had made a great discovery when he found a bronze cannon on the seabed.

The experts said it was a fluke find but he set out to prove them wrong.

e

Perhaps because we specialise in economy flights and package holidays to South America. We're unbeatable on North America and very good on the Caribbean too (unlike many travel agents, our directors have actually been there). We can offer special group departures, concessionary prices, A.B.C.'s, APEX etc. Also one way fares.

h

Bastia, Sept 27.—Max Simeoni, the Corsican guerrilla leader, surrendered here today after more than a year in hiding.

M Simeoni disappeared after guerrillas seeking Corsican autonomy blew up a wine warehouse and fought a gun battle with police in August 1976.

j

BLONDE model Lyndsay Oliver told yesterday of her secret nights of love with rock superstar Rod Stewart . . . and her shock when she lost out to Bianca Jagger.

b

The existence of an almost perfect method of proving or disproving the paternity of a child has been disclosed at an international congress in Hamburg.

It is based on the examination of between 150 and 170 different factors in the blood, including elements in its protein and enzyme content, which are now known to be hereditary.

c

THE Black Parents Movement and Black Students Movement have issued a statement complaining about Miss C——, Headmistress of H—— School for Girls, demanding her resignation. The statement complained 'about Miss C—— preventing pupils from taking exams without proper cause, making life a misery for parents and students, refusing girls references, locking up girls in the cupboard for days and weeks, keeping them in the corridor outside her room for days and even weeks, and all this without schoolwork'.

f

FUNERAL workers on the picket line at Manor Park in East London, in support of their claim for a decent wage.

g

1. The Bicycle v. The Cheque Book

This is a bicycle. Equipped with this and a large amount of cash, you can happily pedal around your own home town and pay your bills. Apart from being enjoyable, the exercise should improve your figure. **The Cheque Book.** With a cheque book you can pay all your bills by post, cutting out boring queues and unnecessary journeys. You may get fat, but you will be happy.

i

This May Hurt a Little

1

Lover's chance

2

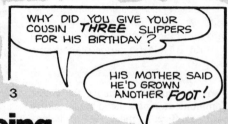

Stop soaring costs going through your roof

3

4

Don't be a doormat

5

A woman's worth...

6

Skipper quits—but he still hopes to play for England

7

'IT'LL MAKE A MAN OF YOU'

8

IS YOUR LIFE AS PRIVATE AS YOU THINK IT IS?

9

The artist and the onlooker

10

How odd we British are. We are world famous for our "reserve". We are far more inclined than the French or the Italians to live our lives behind closed doors, and we are less likely than the Americans to welcome strangers into our homes. Yet we allow ourselves to be spied upon a lot more freely than our European or American neighbours.

a

The early days of a revolution are a time of pervasive confusion. A sense of sweeping change exhilarates some people, frightens others and causes nearly all to question anxiously just what the changes eventually will mean for the shape and texture of their own lives. So it was in Week 1 of the Reagan revolution in U.S. economic and social policy.

b

PRIVATE X was born in Glasgow, one of a family of seven. He went to the local school where he was in a class of 40.

The harassed teacher didn't care if he did any work or even if he was there, so Private X left school at 15 with a good British education. So he could write in a fashion and his favourite reading was comics.

e

Chef Christopher C____, who tried to slip out of an Edgware Road hotel with his lover hoping to dodge a £250 bill, was given a chance to "sort himself out" when he appeared on remand for reports at Marylebone Court.

C____, 21, of Dove Close, Wecock Farm Estate, Waterlooville, Hants, had pleaded guilty to evading the bill at the London Metropole Hotel.

c

One of the questions that seems to bedevil the relationship between some contemporary artists and their audiences is: how much effort may one reasonably expect from the non-specialist spectator?

f

Do you find it hard to say "no" to persuasive salesmen? Do you seethe inwardly at queue-jumpers or do you stand your ground and tell them angrily to go to the back of the queue? Can you complain to a waiter without fear of embarrassment or do you suffer poor service and bad food in silence? Can you pay and accept compliments without feeling self-conscious? Do you frequently find yourself accepting unreasonable work loads in the office, or allow your mother-in-law to blackmail you into doing something you don't want to do?

d

The first strike in America about the sex discrimination issue of "comparable worth," is taking place in the "feminist capital of the world," San Jose, California.

The city has a woman mayor, deputy mayor, town clerk, deputy city manager, labour director, and housing director, and a seven to four female majority on the council. A city spokesman claimed this was why the Municipal Employees' Union has picked on San Jose for the strike.

g

The most crucial bill facing most families each week or month, the one they feel they must pay no matter what, is the one that keeps a roof over their heads

h

SUSAN SPENCER
WEMBLEY PARK

i

IAN BOTHAM'S troubled 12-match reign as England's captain came to an end last night at Lord's, cricket's headquarters.

He walked away from the presentation ceremony at the end of the drawn second Cornhill Test against Australia to resign — unaware that he had already been sacked.

While he was making up his mind to quit at one end of the pavilion during the morning, the selectors were meeting at the other, on the balcony of the players' dining-room to choose his successor.

j

DEDUCTION PUZZLES

Intensive reading and speaking practice. Read the puzzles and answer the questions to find the solution.

The parachutes

Not long ago a man kidnapped a little boy and hid him in the woods. He sent his parents a ransom note telling them to leave him ten thousand pounds in large notes in an airport locker. They were then to wait four hours and go to the locker. In it they would find directions to where their child was. He said that unless they left him the money, they would not see the child for a long time.

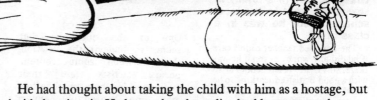

He had thought about taking the child with him as a hostage, but decided against it. He knew that the police had become good at trapping people who had hostages with them.

At the appointed time, he went to the airport and found the money in the locker. He had just enough time to leave the directions and run. The police were close behind him. He boarded the nearest plane and forced the pilot to take off before he was caught.

Knowing that the police would be waiting for him when the plane landed, he came up with a brilliant idea to save himself. He demanded that the hostess should give him two parachutes. He took her with him to the back exit door of the plane and waited several minutes. Then he put one of the parachutes on and jumped alone from the plane. In this way he managed to escape.

The question is, why did he demand two parachutes?

1 What would've happened if he'd stayed on the plane?

2 Did he have a chance of escaping if he jumped safely?

3 Did he have a better chance of escaping if he had a hostage with him?

4 Why?

5 Say you were the hostess. If he'd asked you for two parachutes and taken you with him to the exit door, what would you have thought?

6 What kind of parachutes would you have given him?

7 Why?

The lawyers

There were two lawyers, Alfred and Bertram. Alfred once borrowed a great deal of money from Bertram. He promised to pay him back on the day he won his first case in court. But Alfred was lazy and never took on a case.

At first Bertram didn't mind, but after five years he got tired of waiting for his money. He decided to take Alfred to court to get the money back.

On the day of the trial they both came to the court feeling happy and confident. They shook each other's hand as if nothing was wrong. Alfred was sure that whether he won or lost in court he wouldn't need to pay Bertram the money back. Bertram, on the other hand, was sure he'd get his money back. Can both of them have been right?

A Look at it from Alfred's point of view:

1 If the judge says he must pay, then he has
   a won the case.
   b lost the case.

2 If so, then according to his promise to Bertram,
   a he has to pay Bertram.
   b he needn't pay him.

3 If the judge says he needn't pay Bertram, then he has
   a won the case.
   b lost the case.

4 If so, then according to the law,
   a he must pay Bertram.
   b he needn't pay him.

B Look at it from Bertram's point of view:

1 If the judge says Alfred must pay then he, Bertram, has
   a won the case.
   b lost the case.

2 The judge's ruling is law, so
   a Alfred has to pay up.
   b he doesn't have to pay up.

3 If the judge says Alfred needn't pay then he, Bertram,
   a has won the case.
   b has lost the case.

4 Therefore, according to Alfred's promise,
   a Alfred must pay him.
   b Alfred needn't pay him.

C Does this sound quite right to you? Is either of them right? Where is the contradiction?

The four babies

Anna, Bernard, Carmen and Diana, three girls and a boy, were all recently born in the same maternity hospital. One day all four of their mothers asked a nurse to give them each a bath, because visiting hours were soon to start. Unfortunately the nurse was new. She took off their identification bracelets one by one as she bathed them, but forgot to put any of them on again.

She knew exactly two things about each baby, but she was in such a panic that they got all mixed up in her mind.

Only one of the babies has a lot of hair but it isn't Anna or Carmen.

One of the babies cries all the time but Anna is a happy baby.

One baby always quietly sucks his thumb in his cot but has no hair at all.

The baby who cries a lot has a tiny birthmark by her right ear, but she isn't the smallest baby.

The fattest baby has no hair, hardly cries at all, and doesn't yet realize that her fingers fit in her mouth.

The baby with the fuzzy red hair rarely cries but certainly kicks a lot.

Can the nurse work out which baby is which before another nurse comes along and tells her off?

1 How many of the babies are boys?

2 If the nurse hadn't been in such a panic, should she have known which baby Bernard was straightaway?

3 Has Bernard's hair started to grow yet?

4 Which baby already has a lot of hair and what colour is it?

5 What's the second thing the nurse knows about the baby with a lot of hair?

6 If Anna is the happy baby, can she be the baby who cries a lot?

7 Who must be the cry-baby then?

8 What else does the nurse remember about her?

9 Who's the fattest baby of them all?

10 Now describe each of the babies.

The shipwrecked man

There are three men on an island. They all look the same but one of them is not a native of the island. The one who is not a native was shipwrecked on the island years before. One day a ship comes to look for the shipwrecked man. The people on the ship must decide which of the three men is the shipwrecked man. They can ask the three men only two questions. They know that the shipwrecked man always tells the truth and the natives always tell lies.

They ask the first man, 'Are you the shipwrecked man?' But his answer blows away on the wind and they do not hear it. They ask the second man, 'Did the first man say yes?' He answers, 'Yes.'

From just this much information, they are able to find their man. How?

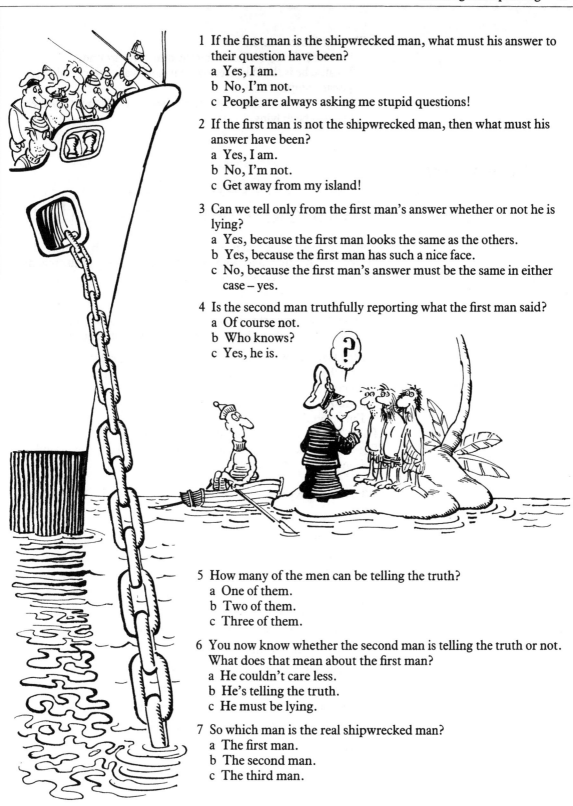

1 If the first man is the shipwrecked man, what must his answer to their question have been?
  a Yes, I am.
  b No, I'm not.
  c People are always asking me stupid questions!

2 If the first man is not the shipwrecked man, then what must his answer have been?
  a Yes, I am.
  b No, I'm not.
  c Get away from my island!

3 Can we tell only from the first man's answer whether or not he is lying?
  a Yes, because the first man looks the same as the others.
  b Yes, because the first man has such a nice face.
  c No, because the first man's answer must be the same in either case – yes.

4 Is the second man truthfully reporting what the first man said?
  a Of course not.
  b Who knows?
  c Yes, he is.

5 How many of the men can be telling the truth?
  a One of them.
  b Two of them.
  c Three of them.

6 You now know whether the second man is telling the truth or not. What does that mean about the first man?
  a He couldn't care less.
  b He's telling the truth.
  c He must be lying.

7 So which man is the real shipwrecked man?
  a The first man.
  b The second man.
  c The third man.

8 The third man is in the story
   a because he's always following the other two around.
   b because he is the shipwrecked man and is always watching for passing ships.
   c because he would have been the shipwrecked man if the other two had been lying.

The murderers

New York, from our own correspondent

Police arrested five men suspected of shooting and killing Richard K. Foxy, the well-known nightclub owner. They now know which of the five men is the killer.

Each man made two statements during the questioning, one of which was true and one false. Here are the five statements:

Daddy Long-Legs 'I didn't kill Foxy. Square-Head murdered him.'
Shorty 'I sure never shot that guy. These other four all say they're innocent.'
Square-Head 'Just look at that guy's face: Big-Nose shot Foxy dead. I'm not guilty.'
Fatty 'Square-Head's the guilty one. I'm innocent.'
Big-Nose 'I had nothing whatever to do with this murder. Daddy Long-Legs and Fatty are the killers.'

Who killed Foxy?

1 How many men were arrested?
2 How many of them deny killing Foxy?
3 How many must be telling the truth when they say they are innocent?
4 How many of them accuse one of the others of the murder?
5 Which man doesn't accuse another man of the killing?
6 What does that man say about the others?
7 Do the others all really say this?
8 So is that man's second statement true?
9 What does Shorty say about himself?
10 Can both his first and second statements be true?
11 Then is his first statement true or false?
12 Who is guilty?

The scientists and the watches

One night, a crazy scientist got involved in a rather silly argument with a fellow scientist. They were arguing about whose watch was the better, the Swiss one or the Japanese one. Being scientists, they decided to do an experiment to test the watches. The first part of the test was to see if both were waterproof. (They were both so convinced of the quality of their watches that they were willing to risk ruining them.)

They went into their laboratory looking very serious. They filled the sink with water, put the watches in, waited impatiently for ten minutes and took them out.

They could see there was something wrong with both watches, but being cautious men of science they observed them for a couple of hours before speaking to each other. The tension was unbearable. They both silently realized that the Swiss watch was losing sixty minutes an hour and the Japanese one double that.

The scientist with the Japanese watch then slowly raised his head and said, 'Both watches are now defective but my watch is right more often than yours, so it's better.' The scientist with the Swiss watch left the room without saying a word.

Was the man with the Japanese watch right? If so, how?

1 What were they arguing about at the beginning of the story?

2 Why couldn't they go on with the experiment after they took the watches out of the water?

3 What did they do for a couple of hours?

4 What did they realize the Swiss watch was doing?

5 If the Swiss watch was losing sixty minutes in sixty minutes, was it
   a going forwards?
   b stopped?
   c going backwards?

6 So how often in every 12-hour period would the Swiss watch show the right time?
   a Once.
   b Twice.

7 How many minutes was the Japanese watch losing every hour?

8 If a watch loses 120 minutes every sixty minutes, is it
   a going forwards?
   b stopped?
   c going backwards?

9 How often in every 12-hour period will the Japanese watch show
   the correct time?
   a Once.
   b Twice.

10 Was the scientist right when he said, 'But my watch is right more
    often than yours'?

11 Why is this absurd?

The sultan and the cheat

A sultan ordered ten goldsmiths to make ten coins each. Each coin
was to weigh exactly ten grams of pure gold.

One of the goldsmiths was a bad man. He decided to cheat. He
made all his ten coins one gram short. Now the sultan heard that one
of the goldsmiths had cheated. He also heard that this man had made
each of his coins one gram short.

The sultan was a very clever person. He took a certain number of
coins from each of the smiths, weighed them together once only and
found their weight to be 540 grams. This was enough for him to find
out which one of the goldsmiths had cheated.

How did he do it and who was the cheat?

1 How many goldsmiths were there?

2 How many of them were cheats?

3 The cheat, like the others, made ten coins. How many grams
   short was each coin?

4 Did the sultan find the cheat
   a by looking each man in the eye?
   b by weighing coins?
   c by asking his mother?

5 How many times did he weigh the coins he took from them?

6 Did he take the coins to weigh from
   a one goldsmith?
   b some of the goldsmiths?
   c all of them?

7 Suppose he had taken all ten coins from each smith and put them
   together on the scales. When he weighed them how many grams
   short would they have been?

8 Would he have known that one of the smiths had cheated?

9 Would he have known which smith had cheated?

10 Suppose he took one coin from the first smith, two coins from the

second and three from the third, how many would he take from the others?

11 How many coins would that be altogether?

12 If nobody had cheated, what should the total weight of these coins have been?
   a 500 grams?
   b 550 grams?
   c 600 grams?

13 How much did the coins he put on the scale actually weigh?
14 So how many of the coins on the scale were made by the cheat?
15 Who was the cheat?

The prisoners

The king of an unnamed country never tries his prisoners in a courtroom. Instead, he puts them to a test which he makes up himself. During a riot in the capital, three men were taken prisoner and brought to the king. This was the test he devised. He had the prisoners blindfolded and taken to a field where there were five poles, three white and two black. The poles were in a straight line from east to west. The prisoners were tied to the three poles nearest the west. All three were facing west. When the blindfolds were removed, each prisoner could see only the poles in front of him.

The king said, 'If one of you can tell me the colour of the pole he is tied to, I will set all three of you free. If none of you can tell me, you will have to stay in prison for ten years. If any of you guesses wrong, you will all be shot. There are three white poles and two black ones.

I will now ask each of you if he can tell the colour of his pole. You may answer only yes or no or that you don't know.'

The king asked Prisoner X first, Y second, and Z third. Each heard the others' answers. What did each prisoner answer when his turn came? Were they set free?

1 How many poles could X see?

2 What colour were they?

3 If X had seen two black poles instead, what would he have known

4 As it was, what answer did X give the king?

5 When Y heard X's answer, he knew X had not seen two black poles. There are two other colour combinations X might have seen, Y thinks. What are they?

6 What colour pole could Y see?

7 Could Y tell whether his pole was black or white?

8 When the king asked him, what did he have to say?

9 When Z heard Y's answer, he had to think hard and fast. Like Y, he realized that X had not seen two black poles. So Z knew that at most only one of the two poles (his and Y's) could be . . . what colour?

10 Z also knew this: if Y had seen that Z's pole was black, Y would've known his own pole was . . . what colour? But Y didn't.

11 Did Z know the colour of his pole?

12 What happened to the three prisoners?

Four women

In a remote mountain village in the East, there is always one wise woman who is both feared and respected by her people. From the time she is chosen until her death she plays a very important part in the lives of the villagers. When she feels her death is near, she calls her four apprentices to her house to choose her successor. Her test has been a secret for many generations.

The four women are asked to sit around a table. The wise woman tells them to close their eyes tightly and cover them with their hands. She then tells them she is going to put a mark on each of their foreheads. The mark may be either white or black. Then she marks them and tells them to open their eyes. They look at each others' foreheads. Any woman who sees more black than white marks must stand up. The first woman who can say what colour mark is on her own forehead becomes the successor.

The last time the test took place, all four women stood up. No one spoke for what seemed a long time. Finally one of the women identified her mark.

What was her reasoning?

1 The women were told to stand up only if . . .?

2 How many of the women stood up?

3 So how many of them saw more black than white marks?

4 If the wise woman had made three white marks and one black, how many would have stood up?

5 Suppose she'd made two white and two black marks. Would anyone have stood up? Which ones?

6 If she'd made one white mark and three black, would any of them have stood up? How many?

7 What if she'd made four black marks?

8 So which of the possible colour combinations could be the right one?

9 Would all four women have realized this when they saw that all of them were standing up?

10 If one of the marks was white, which of the women would've seen it?

11 What would they have known about their own marks then?

12 Wouldn't all three of them have said this immediately then?

13 Did any of them say anything?

14 So could any of them have seen a white mark?

15 When one of them spoke, what had she realized and what did she say?

Follow Up

1 Since no-one had a white mark, did all of them have an equal chance?

2 If one had had a white mark, would she have had an equal chance?

3 What other colour combination could the wise woman have used to make it a fair test?

4 Is this a good test of wisdom?

5 What, if anything, would you use it for?

PSYCHOLOGY QUESTIONNAIRES

Reading and discussion. Answer the questions with 'yes', 'no' or 'it depends', giving reasons if you wish. Then read out some of your answers to the class, and discuss.

Embarrassment

Do you get embarrassed . . .

1 If you see your zip is down and people have noticed.

2 If someone uses words you think are dirty in public.

3 If you are out with a child and it's very quiet and the child makes a scene.

4 If your children use dirty words in front of people who would disapprove.

5 If your parents, spouse or girlfriend/boyfriend start shouting at you in public.

6 When you've forgotten to go somewhere you were invited and they phone afterwards to ask where you were.

7 If you are caught lying.

8 When someone compliments you profusely.

9 If people pay a lot of attention to you or fuss over you.

10 If you've been watching a nice-looking man/woman in public and they speak to you.

11 If you are trying to refuse an invitation with a white lie.

12 If your boss reprimands you in front of other workers.

13 If someone asks you a very personal question.

14 If you've been trying to chat someone up and they are rude about it.

15 If you have to make a speech in front of a large group.

16 If you want to make a statement or ask a question after a lecture or speech.

17 When you want to complain about something in a restaurant or shop or at work.

18 When you are criticized.

19 While you are trying to criticize someone else.

20 If you suddenly realize you are making a fool of yourself or have said the wrong thing.

21 If someone is obviously trying to fix you up with a friend of theirs.

22 If you know or think people are talking about you.

23 If people come to visit unexpectedly and your house is a mess.

24 If you are going somewhere with a group and someone the group doesn't like asks to come along.

25 If you find you haven't got enough money with you to pay for a meal or stand a round at the pub.

26 If you break something in a shop.

27 If you spill or break something in someone else's house.

28 If you arrive very late for something important.

29 If you've been invited somewhere with someone. They say yes but later they don't want to go. You have to explain when you arrive why they aren't coming.

30 If you arrive at a party or dinner or meeting wearing the wrong type of clothes.

Laughter

Do you laugh . . .

1 When you get embarrassed.
2 When you don't know what to say.
3 When you don't think it's funny but someone wants you to laugh.
4 When you are tense and need relief from it.
5 If someone slips on something or is clumsy.
6 When someone else feels embarrassed.
7 At a joke about other religions.
8 At a joke about other nationalities.
9 When someone makes a fool of themselves.
10 When someone tries to do something they aren't good at.
11 When a child cries over something you think is unimportant.
12 When someone makes fun of a third person.
13 At practical jokes played on other people.
14 At people's physical characteristics.
15 At dirty jokes.

16 At jokes about people with physical or mental handicaps.
17 At a person dressed up or made up strangely.
18 At pornographic and other sexual references.
19 At sarcastic remarks.
20 At things you disagree with or don't understand.
21 When someone burps loudly.
22 When someone is clowning.
23 More than usual when tired or drunk.
24 At really stupid jokes.
25 If you are reading or thinking something funny in a bus or walking down a road.
26 When someone makes fun of you.
27 When someone plays a practical joke on you.
28 At your own jokes.
29 Because other people are laughing.
30 When someone tickles you.

Tears

In the following circumstances, would you cry?

1 Someone you know has died.
2 You hurt yourself.
3 You're frightened.
4 You feel very nervous and tense.
5 You feel totally frustrated.
6 You've been laughing too hard.
7 Someone is angry at you and shouts.
8 Someone criticizes you harshly.

9 You're caught doing something you know is wrong.
10 Someone is trying to make you feel bad.
11 You feel very ill.
12 You see someone you haven't seen for a long time.
13 You move out of a neighbourhood you like.
14 Someone you love is going away for a long time.

15 You're by yourself and feeling lonely.

16 At the end of a love relationship which you have ended.

17 At the end of a love relationship which the lover has ended.

18 In a sad film.

19 In a very moving film – even if it ends happily.

20 At the news of a terrible tragedy.

21 On your birthday.

22 You hear or sing national anthems.

23 You hear or sing political songs you agree with.

24 Your children leave home.

25 At weddings.

26 Your pet dies.

27 You peel onions.

28 A national leader or hero is killed.

29 The anniversary of someone's death.

30 You receive an honour or award publicly.

Fear

Would you feel afraid if . . .

1 You woke up in the middle of a nightmare.

2 You were driving and just missed having a fatal accident.

3 You found yourself falling from a high window.

4 You were going to lose your job.

5 Your child was very seriously ill.

6 A policeman stopped you and you didn't know what for.

7 Your doctor told you you had three months left to live.

8 You came under fire for the first time.

9 You were burgling a house.

10 You had to go to consult a psychiatrist.

11 You were coming up to retirement age.

12 You were in high mountains and you had to cross white water in a wooden box suspended from a cable.

13 You had to sleep in a (haunted) house alone.

14 You had failed to do a job you had promised someone you would do.

15 You were going to be sterilized.

16 You knew your marriage was breaking up.

17 Your child was out very late and you couldn't locate her/him.

18 You had a dentist appointment in ten minutes.

19 The doctor said you needed an operation.

20 You had to live alone.

21 Your exams were coming up soon.

22 You were walking down a dark city street and someone stepped out of the shadows in front of you.

23 You were alone at home and suddenly you heard a loud noise downstairs.

24 A black cat crossed your path.

25 You were climbing a steep mountain.

26 Your boat was sinking.

27 A dog ran at you in the street growling.

28 If you were told you/your girlfriend were pregnant.

29 You received a telegram late at night.

30 You saw a robbery taking place.

Silence

Would you stay silent if . . .

1 You didn't understand a question you had been asked.

2 You had been accused of stealing something.

3 Someone asked your opinion.

4 Someone shouted at you.

5 You were in pain.

6 Someone insulted you.

7 Someone misunderstood what you had said.

8 Someone told you a joke you didn't approve of.

9 Everybody in a meeting disagreed with your ideas.

10 You hated someone.

11 You were in a crowd of shouting people.

12 You suddenly went deaf.

13 You were having a baby.

14 You were in solitary confinement.

15 You had emotionally hurt someone you loved.

16 You were told you had passed an important exam.

17 You knew an unpleasant but important fact about someone.

18 Someone was chasing you down a dark street.

19 A person wasn't doing something very well but you wanted him/her to learn independently.

20 You were given bad food in a restaurant.

21 You were being tortured for information.

22 You found someone had lied to you.

23 You wanted a chatterbox to shut up.

24 Someone said they wanted to marry you.

25 Someone told you to shut up.

26 You were asked to report a friend who had done something wrong.

27 Someone asked you for money in the street.

28 Someone spoke to you on a train and you didn't like their looks.

29 You saw a parent hit a child in the street.

30 You saw someone was about to light the wrong end of a cigarette.

ROLE-PLAY THE NEWS

Role-play. In groups of three or four, read the newspaper articles and then act out the stories.

The lady was a tramp

The secret life of sea-side tramp Stella M—— was revealed yesterday.

For the frail, raggedly dressed woman, who slept in a tent in an alleyway until she died of exposure last year, was worth ... £33,000.

She was also a qualified vet and a property owner. But Stella – she was 49 when she died – turned her back on the good life to become a tramp in Eastbourne, Sussex.

A supermarket worker who knew Stella said last night, 'She was a lovely woman, well-spoken and well-educated. Apparently she had a chest illness

some years ago and doctors advised her to get into the open air more often. She must have taken them at their word.'

Whose baby?

Mr and Mrs Jones both wanted a child but they had tried unsuccessfully to have a baby for five years. Tests indicated that there was nothing wrong with her eggs or his sperm so the doctor took an egg from Mrs Jones and some sperm from Mr Jones and put them together in his laboratory. When the foetus started growing he implanted it in Mrs French, who was Mrs Jones's sister. She had agreed to carry the baby.

When the baby was born nine months later, Mrs Jones took it home and looked after it.

Whose baby was it?

Publican jailed for assault

Brian S——, aged 38, a publican at M—— was found guilty at Bristol Crown Court yesterday of assaulting a 'gentle tax man' who was removing bar furniture as payment of an outstanding £228 tax debt.

Mr S—— was sentenced to three months' imprisonment for an assault on Mr David T——, aged 42, a tax collector. Mr and Mrs S—— had both denied causing bodily harm to Mr T—— at their public house on June 15.

Helicopter 'defeats driving ban'

Mr Frank M——, aged 32, intends to use a helicopter to commute the 10 miles between the garage which he owns and his home on a farm, a journey he used to make in his Ferrari.

Mr J——, the local M.P., said yesterday, 'There is something wrong if a man can defeat a driving ban because he can afford to buy a helicopter and learn to fly it.' Mr M—— was entitled to his actions but the driving ban would not affect him as much as it would most people.

Mr M—— was banned for 12 months for speeding. Before the hearing, he bought a three-seat helicopter and moved an instructor into his home.

The refugee

There was a *coup d'état* in Country A. John escaped to Country B, as the army were looking for him in Country A.

In Country B he went to see a friend to ask for help. He had no money and nowhere to stay. The friend was cold to him. He gave him £20 and asked him not to come back because he was frightened of trouble.

Next morning John went to meet the leader of his party. The leader had also escaped to Country B. John asked him for help. The leader refused. He said, 'You did not obey the Party – we will not help you.'

John hated the Catholic Church. He had always hated it since his childhood. That night he had nowhere to sleep. He walked into a Catholic church and asked the priest if he could sleep in his house. The priest said yes. He gave him dinner and promised John a room as long as he needed one.

Next morning John got up and threw himself into the river.

The bicycle

A teacher had a beautiful black bike. One day he rode it to the school where he taught and put it in the bicycle shed. He carefully padlocked the bike.

A thief went into the school bike shed during classes and sawed through the padlock on the teacher's bike. He rode it to a shop where he sold it to the shopman for £5.

The shopman cleaned the bike and oiled it. Later that day a student from the school came into the shop looking for a second-hand bike to buy. The shopman sold him the stolen bike for £30.

Next day the student rode the bike to school and left it in the school shed. He did not padlock it.

As the teacher was leaving school he saw *his* bike back in the shed. He was very, very happy. As he was wheeling it out of the bike shed, he ran into the student.

Sabotage at factory was third incident

The sabotaging of a welding machine at the M—— car component factory at B——, was the third such incident in a week, a senior union official said yesterday.

A welder escaped injury on Monday when an explosion occurred as he switched on his machine. A piece of wire had been used to bridge two terminals.

Sixty electricians are sitting in at the factory because of a dis-pute over payment for time when they were laid off. They have denied tampering with the welding machine.

Sacked

Sally taught drama to 9–11 year-old children in a primary school. She was also a very active member of a political party. One time the parents of one of her pupils saw her on a demonstra-tion.

They told several of the other parents and a few of them phoned the school to protest. The headmistress didn't like it very much but she did nothing. As Sally was an excellent teacher, the headmistress didn't want to lose her so she soothed the parents' feelings.

Some time later there was a three-day demo and Sally went on it the first two days. The third day, which was a school day, she brought it up in class because she felt it was stupid to spend so much time on some-thing and then not bring it up. The class discussed the prob-lems that had led to the demo and then dramatized it – very well, she thought.

That day, after school, quite a few from that class decided on their own to go to the demo to see what was happening. Parents who usually came to meet their children or who expected them to come home directly after school got very worried and upset. When they learnt where their children had been, they got furious. They rang the school the next day, one after the other, and complained. One or two of them were influential local people. The headmistress felt she had no choice. She sacked Sally.

LIES, ALL LIES!

Spot the lies!

Read the passages and uncover the lies. Then explain them to your group or class.

Come South!

Amnesia is a young, active country which welcomes young, active people. If you come to our country, we want you to be happy from the word 'go'. We are ready to spend money, a lot of money, to make sure you settle in easily and fast.

To give you an example: in 1976 the Amnesian government spent huge sums on the settlement of immigrants. The money spent was equivalent to the annual income of all the people living in the shaded areas of the map. What more could you ask for?

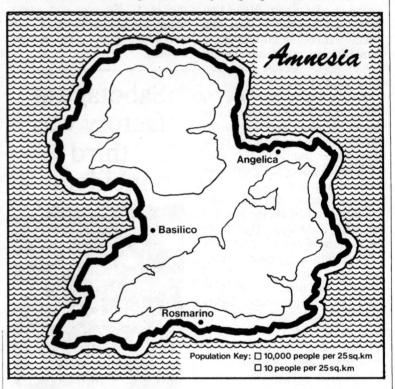

'No time to go to school'

Nine-year-old Susie refuses to go to school. She says she hasn't got time. This is how she proved it:

'There are 365 days in a year. I sleep eight hours a day so we have to subtract 122 days for sleeping. I eat three times a day and it takes about an hour each time, so we have to subtract 45 days for that. From the remaining 198 days, take away 90 for summer holidays and 21 for Christmas and Easter holidays. That leaves only 87 days for going to school but we haven't yet talked about Saturdays and Sundays.'

Keep off the roads!

Thirty years ago only 200 people were killed on the roads of this country in a year.

Now the appalling total is 10,000 per annum. And the killer? The motor car!

From these figures it is clear that the motor car today is fifty times more dangerous than it was thirty years ago.

So keep out of the driving seat – keep off the roads! (If you value your life, that is.)

Union wants 50% increase in wages

Mr Don S——, workers' representative at the M—— plant in Liverpool, told his men they should demand a 50% rise. 'Last year,' he said, 'the management forced a 50% reduction in our wage packets. We must fight and fight and fight to regain all we have lost. We must, this year, demand nothing less than a 50% increase.'

Cheaper and cheaper!

Inflation has been going up and up. Prices have risen by 10% over the last six months. But not OUR prices! They have fallen steeply in the same period. *How* steeply you can see from the graph.

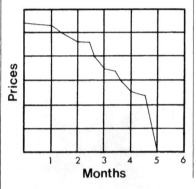

Bungalows for sale

Do you find London too cold in winter and too hot in summer?

If you want to avoid extremes, spend your next holidays in our ideal bungalows at Tassili, Northern Sahara. The average temperature in Tassili is a pleasant 28 degrees centigrade.

And only four hours from hot and cold London by air.

Crime wave

More and more crimes are being reported in the city's daily papers. People are getting more and more frightened. They are demanding immediate action. So much newspaper space is taken up with crimes that the Police Commissioner is seriously embarrassed. He has promised to act quickly to reduce the number of crimes.

Join up!

Join the army and see the world. Even if you are sent to an active area like Northern Ireland you will be safer than if you go on living in London, Manchester or Glasgow.

This can be proved scientifically: the death rate among troops in Northern Ireland last year was 2 per 1000. The death rate among the civilian population of London for the same period was 16 per 1000. Join the army and escape an early death.

What is it?

Read the passage and decide what the object is.

Cut price central heating

Unaffected by rising fuel costs. No need for double windows. Keeps you and your children warm inside the house and out. Just right first thing on a frosty morning.

For Sale

Has crossed the Sahara, never boiled once. One owner. Four years old. Ideal for long distance journey in arid country. Spare wheel unnecessary. Ample luggage carrying capacity. Unlimited mileage per gallon. Price: £200, or nearest offer.

House Agent's Advertisement

'Mon Repos' is situated in the valley of the river Tesk and has a pleasant view over farm land.

'Mon Repos' is suitable for a couple with one or two children and is within easy reach of the shops and a mainline station.

The property is in good repair both inside and out.

Special features: its round windows make this a most distinctive home, as does the fact that the southern end of the property is pointed.

Ideal for an owner who does not want to spend his time cutting grass – no land goes with the property.

For Sale

Cheap at the price – will store up to 100 kilos of meat. Unaffected by power cuts. Everybody needs one for handy storage purposes. People only need to try our product once. Stock up in time. Seasoned oak.

What is a lie?

Read the passage and answer the questions.

1 A girl went out to buy ice-creams for herself and her younger sister. On the way back from the ice-cream van she dropped one of them. She opened her front door and went into the house happily licking the remaining ice-cream.

'I'm sorry, but I dropped yours on the ground,' she told her little sister.

Did she lie? If not, what did she do? Have you ever acted like the elder sister? If so, describe the situation, and what you said.

2 A boy couldn't draw very well but he desperately wanted to be able to draw well. One day he pinched another child's drawing book and took it home.

'I did that drawing,' he told his mother.

Was the boy a liar? Who was he lying to? If you were his mother and found out, what would you do?

3 A boy was playing ball when he broke a neighbour's window. When his mother accused him of doing it, the boy said, 'I didn't break the window, John did.'

Why did the boy lie in that way? Have you ever told lies like this? Give examples.

4 **Girl** Mummy, can I have an ice-cream?
Mother No, certainly not, not before your lunch.
Girl (*goes upstairs to father*) Daddy, can I have an ice-cream?
Father Have you asked your mother?
Girl Yes, Daddy, I have.
Father OK, then, I suppose you can have one.

Did the little girl say anything that was untrue? Did she intend to tell a lie? If you were this little girl's parents and you found her out, what would you do and why?

5 There was a chalk fight in a school classroom during break. John picked up the board rubber and threw it at his friend. He missed and broke a window. The teacher came in a few minutes later and asked, 'Who broke that window?' John said nothing.

Was John a liar? Who was responsible for the breaking of the window? Have you ever been in this sort of situation? What happened?

6 Ms Schmidt wanted a job as a bi-lingual secretary. The interviewer asked her, 'Ms Schmidt, have you taken the Cambridge Proficiency Examination in English?' Ms Schmidt replied, 'Yes.' She had failed the exam the year before.

Was Ms Schmidt lying? What would you have done in her place? Have you ever been in this sort of position?

Questionnaire: When do you lie?

1 Someone rings up and invites you to a boring party.

Do you: a tell them the party would bore you?
         b invent an excuse?
         c do something else?

2 You are a doctor. Your patient is dying of cancer.

Do you: a tell the patient s/he's got only a short time to live?
         b lie to the patient?
         c do something else?

3 You have broken the speed limit. The police stop you.

Do you: a admit you have broken the speed limit?
         b deny you have broken the limit?
         c do something else?

4 You are seventeen and you find you are pregnant.

Do you: a tell your parents?
         b say nothing to them?
         c do something else?

5 You are hitch-hiking. A driver picks you up. He says he has just stolen the car.

Do you: a report him to the police?
         b do nothing?
         c do something else?

6 You are bringing twenty bottles of whisky home from abroad. The customs officer asks you, 'Do you have anything to declare?'

Do you: a say yes?
         b say no?
         c say something else?

7 Your child lies to you; you find him/her out.

Do you: a tell him/her lying is wicked?
         b tell him/her lying is stupid if one is caught?
         c do something else?

8 You miss a morning at work because you went shopping. Your boss asks where you were.

Do you: a tell the truth?
         b say you were ill?
         c do something else.

MORAL ISSUES

Intensive reading. Read the passages and think through the problems.

Laying-off You are the manager of a small company. Your company has been selling less of its products recently. You have decided that the only thing to do is to lay off one of your staff. (There is no recognized way of doing this and you do not have to make redundancy payments in your country.) Which one of these people will you sack?

Jill   is an irregular time-keeper but when she is on form she is probably the best worker you have. She is 30.

Bill   is the foreman. He does very little. The workers like him as a person. He is 50.

Henry   is the shop steward and he keeps the workers quiet by promising action when they get angry, and then doing nothing. He is 45.

Jenny   is not a good worker but she has been with the firm for twenty years. She has eight children. She is 47.

John   is very lazy. He knows one or two things about your private life which you don't want him to tell anyone. He is 24.

David   is left wing. He is aggressive at union meetings. He has a following among the workers. He is a local councillor.

Six months after the sacking, you find that you still haven't solved the problem of falling sales. Will you sack someone else? If not, what other possible courses of action are there?

In court You are a judge. You must decide how long to send the accused to prison for. The minimum is three months. The maximum is a real life sentence. You can also acquit.

Case 1   The accused is a prisoner of war. Your country has just defeated his. He was a pilot. He dropped an atom bomb on your tenth largest city, killing 200,000 people and injuring many more.

Case 2   The accused is a doctor. He gave an overdose to an 85-year-old painter who had terminal cancer. The painter had asked for the overdose. The painter's family accuse the doctor of murder.

Case 3   The accused found her husband in their bed with another woman. She took the breadknife and killed him.

Case 4   This man is a well-known leader of a radical organization. He was recently tried for possessing one marijuana cigarette and sentenced to ten years in prison. He is appealing the decision.

Case 5   This factory owner is on trial for cruel and inhuman treatment. The workers in his factory had a sit-down strike to protest against low wages. The owner set rats loose in the factory. The workers killed all the rats and no one was hurt.

Case 6   This woman was given thalidomide while she was pregnant. She gave birth to a baby without arms and legs. When it was two months old, she smothered it while it was sleeping.

Case 7   a These three teenage boys were having a fight with a fourth boy near a swimming pool. They threw him in the water and then stood on him till he drowned.

b These five adults were sitting not far from the pool and watched the fight. They did nothing and are accused of complicity.

The decision

In battle, a platoon of marines were outnumbered. They had retreated across a bridge over a river, but the enemy were still mostly on the other side. If someone went back to the bridge and blew it up while the enemy were crossing, the company could escape. But the man who blew up the bridge would probably be killed – it is a 4 to 1 chance. The platoon commander has to decide what to do. He asks for volunteers but no one comes forward.

These six courses of action occur to him:

a To go back himself and ask the sergeant to command the platoon. The sergeant has never been in command before.

b To send a man who has a lot of strength and courage, but who is a bad troublemaker in the company. He is always stealing things from the other men, beating them up and refusing to do his work.

c To send a man who has caught a fatal disease in the country. Although he is ill and will probably die in a short time anyway, the man is strong enough to do the job.

d To take the whole platoon back to the bridge to fight it out with the enemy.

e To make everyone in the company, including himself, draw lots to see who must go back.

f Not to send anyone back to the bridge.

Consider these questions:

1 If you were the marine in (b) and the commander told you to go back, what would you do?

2 If you were the marine in (c) how would you feel?

3 If you were in the platoon in (d) how would you feel? Would you go back?

4 If you were a marine in (a) or (f) would you volunteer to go back after the commander told the platoon his decisions?

5 If you were the commander, which choice would you make?

Private Medicine

Private medicine is concerned about the national health

Private medicine is part of the national health. A vital part, it contributes a good deal to the National Health Service. For example, pay beds in NHS hospitals will give 240 million annually to the financially-stretched National Health Service.

But it's not just a matter of money. Private medicine preserves everyone's right to freedom of choice. Some million people choose to go privately when they need treatment. The vast majority are ordinary men and women and their families. They budget for health protection from their earnings through organizations such as ours. What's more, over eight people out of every ten (82%) believe in the right to pay for private medicine.

What's the Government up to? If it doesn't make financial sense and the vast majority don't want it, why are the Government proposing legislation to phase out pay beds and control private medicine? And why do they want to introduce it in advance of the findings of the Royal Commission on Health?

Patients before Politics. A doctor's loyalty is to his patients. That's why the Medical Profession has always shown itself to be completely opposed to any political suggestion that the patient's freedom of choice should be tampered with. Such suggestions are rife today. The issue at stake, is not just one of professional freedom but also of patient freedom.

Now consider these statements:

1 Most people cannot afford to pay for private treatment.
2 If you are a NHS patient, you may have to wait months for a bed in hospital. If you are a private patient, you get a bed very quickly.
3 Many people complain that doctors give too much time to private patients and not enough to NHS patients.
4 Doctors are paid by the National Health Service. They earn extra money from private patients.

Look at the advertisement again. Pick out the statements that are not exactly true and explain why. Is this lying? If so, why? If not, what is it?

Part 3
WRITING AND SPEAKING

CREATIVE DRILLS

Writing and speaking practice. Write sentences, using the patterns given.
Then compare your solutions with those of others in your group or class.

1 Suppose you are very angry with someone you know well, but don't want to say it. How many ways can you think of to show someone you are angry without saying it directly?

   a You can show them by . . .ing . . .
   b You can make it clear by . . .ing . . .
   c You can let them know it by . . .ing . . .
   d By . . .ing . . .

2 My kitchen is swarming with flies! How can I get rid of them?

   a How about . . .ing . . .?
   b What about . . .ing . . .?
   c One way would be to . . .
   d I'd . . .

3 I'm much too shy to tell a certain person I'm in love with them. How can I show it?

   a Why not . . .?
   b Why don't you . . .?
   c Couldn't you . . .?
   d Isn't one way to . . .?

4 I live in a city. I love growing vegetables but I haven't got a garden. Where else could they be grown?

   a They could be . . .
   b You could . . .
   c You might . . .

5 A man has been told by his doctor he must not play chess again. His wife has burnt his chess sets. He would feel guilty to go out and buy a set, so he sets about making one secretly. What could he use and what would the disadvantages be?

   a He could . . . but then he'd have to . . .
   b He could . . . but then they'd . . .
   c He could . . . but then . . . might (not) . . .

6 You have a hard exam to take. You know very little about the subject. Will you pass – or won' you?

   a . . . will/won't . . . if . . .
   b . . . will/won't . . . unless . . .

7 Imagine you are living on the third floor of an old wooden house. You are woken one night by shouting. A fire has broken out on the ground floor and is rapidly spreading to the first floor. How would you escape?

   a If there was/were . . ., I could . . .
   b If I had . . ., I would . . .

8 You are walking down a busy street in your home town. You have a sudden uncontrollable urge to shock people. What would(n't) you do and how would they react?

   a If I . . ., they'd . . .
   b They might well . . . if I . . .
   c I wouldn't . . . because . . .

9 You are a doctor. A patient comes to see you and complains that s/he has spots. First you ask some questions. Then you explain why they have the spots and what to do about them.

   a You'll go on having spots until . . .
   b You have those spots because . . .
   c Your spots won't go away unless . . .

10 You are a doctor. A mother brings you a child of ten that wets its bed every night. Give possible explanations and advice.

   a The bedwetting is probably due to . . .
   b Unless . . . the bedwetting is sure to continue.
   c Until . . ., s/he will probably go on wetting his/her bed.

11 After the Battle of Waterloo in 1815, the English exiled Napoleon to St. Helena, a small island in the South Atlantic. Napoleon did *not* commit suicide. Imagine, however, that he sometimes wanted to. How could he have killed himself?

   a He could've . . . (himself)
   b He might've tried . . .ing . . . (himself)

Now think about ways we might use today, which Napoleon couldn't have used.

   c He couldn't have . . . because . . .

12 You are a psychiatrist. Yesterday your client killed her/his mother and father. You are asking questions to find out why s/he did it.

   a Did you murder them because . . .
   b Did you want to . . .
   c Were you/they . . .
   d Had they/you . . .

13 You come home late from work for the *n*th time. On the way home you need to think up an excuse to tell your husband/wife.

   a I was just going to . . . but then . . .
   b I was on the point of . . . when . . .
   c I intended to . . . but you see . . .
   d I *did* try to . . . but, well, . . .

14 A friend of mine has got so fat he needs help getting out of bed in the morning. They'll have to widen the doors of his flat soon! What should he do?

   a He'd better . . .
   b He ought to . . .
   c He should . . .
   d Tell him . . .

15 Traffic laws are there to prevent accidents and most people obey them most of the time. But sometimes they don't. When?

   A driver will go through red lights if:
   a s/he . . .
   b s/he's . . .
   c s/he's going to . . .
   d s/he wants to . . .

16 You've been out drinking with friends and your children have been waiting for you, getting more and more furious. Make up some excuses they might accept.

   a We've been . . .
   b We tried to . . . but . . .
   c We wanted to . . . but . . .
   d We wouldn't have . . . except that . . .

17 If I told you someone slept on the floor next to his bed, you probably wouldn't believe me. But it's true. Can you think of some good reasons why?

The man slept on the floor next to his bed:
a because he had . . .
b because he was . . .
c because he . . .
d because he was going to . . .

18 In the future, when all babies are grown in test tubes, no one will naturally belong to a family. If you'd been born in a test tube and were looking for parents for yourself, how would you want them to be?

a I'd/I wouldn't want them to . . .
b I'd/I wouldn't expect them to . . .
c They'd have to . . .

19 How much do you know about the people in your class? Think about one of your classmates. Try to imagine what that person used to do as a child.

a S/he used to . . .
b S/he'd . . .
c S/he often . . .

20 There was a mass kidnapping at the airport yesterday. The kidnappers wanted a ransom and they shot a hostage every hour between 12 noon and 11 p.m. When the last hostage was shot, they vanished down a secret tunnel and got away. The police suspect you. Produce an alibi for each of the hours between noon and 11 p.m. yesterday.

At . . . yesterday afternoon/yesterday evening/last night, I was . . .ing with . . . and we were . . .

21 Strikes are hard on workers and their families, so the decision to go on strike is not easily made. In strikes you have heard about, what problems might have stopped them, but didn't?

The workers went on strike:
a although . . .
b even though . . .
c but . . .
d in spite of . . .

22 Up to now, she had refused to pay the money. But when they told her what would happen if she didn't, she changed her mind. Why?

She decided to pay up:
a rather than . . .
b so as not to . . .
c to avoid . . .

CREATIVE CROSSWORDS

Writing practice.

1 Here is a crossword puzzle. You've got to write the clues, like this:

1 *down*	is	a person	who . . .
1 *across*	are	people	that . . .

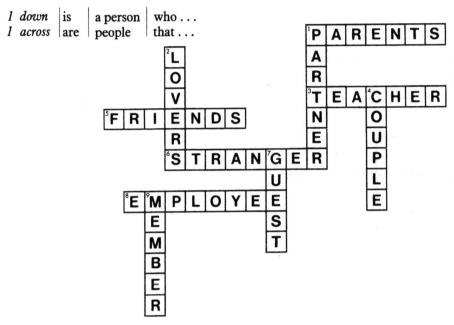

2 Write the clues for this crossword.

1 *down*	is	something	that . . .
3 *across*		a place	where . . .
		a kind of . . .	which . . .

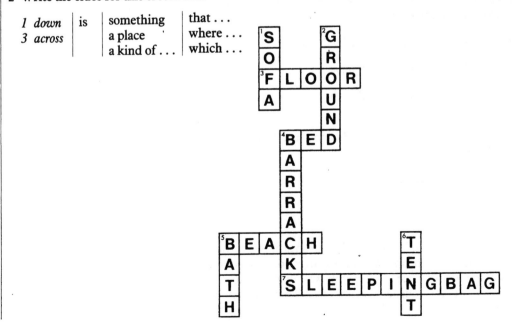

3 In each clue of this crossword, people are having something done by someone else. Who?

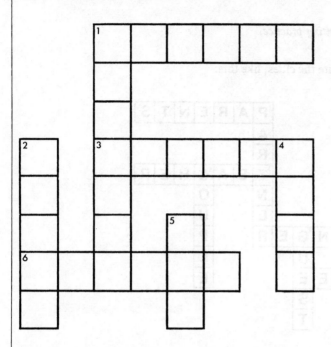

Clues

She wanted to have her bags carried but she couldn't find a *1 across*.

The prime minister didn't want to speak so she had her place at the dinner taken by a local *3 across*.

He went to the *6 across* and had his beard trimmed.

The publisher had the job done by a *1 down*.

The manager wanted to break the strike – he tried to get the work done by *2 down*.

The tourist climbed the mountains of Tibet and had his photo taken by a *4 down*.

They rang a *5 down* and had the calf seen to.

4 Invent your own crossword. Fill a grid like the ones above with, for example, the names of people who have things done to them (e.g. patient, victim, employee) or of people who do things to other people (e.g. doctor, murderer, employer). Then write clues for each name.

WHAT'S IN A BLOT?

*Writing and speaking practice. Look at the blots from every angle.
What can you see? Write sentences. Then criticize each other's
sentences.*

a It's like . . .

b It reminds me of . . .

c It looks like . . .

d I get the impression of . . .

e It gives me the impression of . . .

f It's kind of a . . .

g That might be . . .

h Could it be . . .

1

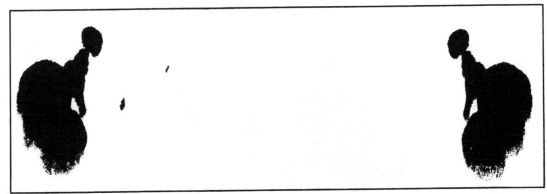

2

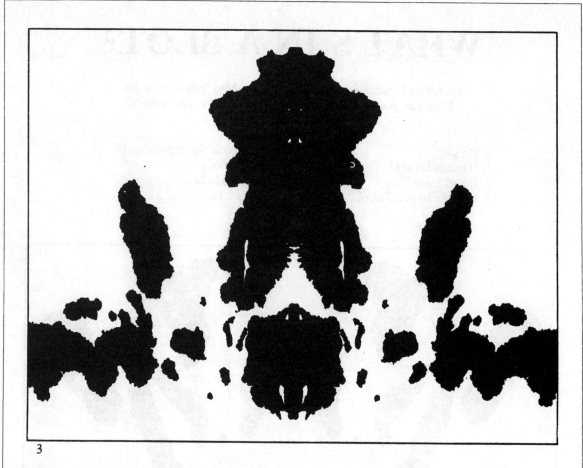

3

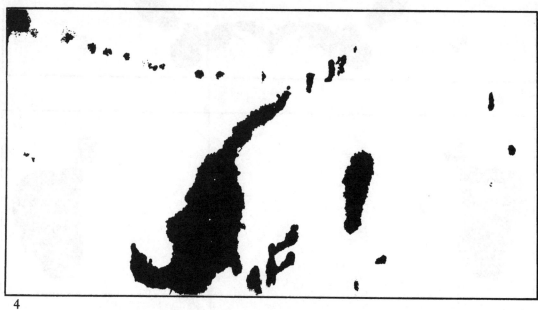

4

DESCRIBE YOURSELF

Writing and speaking practice.

The path game

Write a short paragraph for each of the seven items.

1 You're going along a path – describe the kind of path it is.
2 You find a twig. What sort is it? What do you do with it?
3 A fallen tree trunk is blocking your path. What do you do?
4 You see a bear on the path. What do you do?
5 You come to a fork in the path. What do you do?
6 You come to a wall. Describe it.
7 You hear a sound beyond the wall – what is it?

The survivors

Read the passage and then make a list of the people, starting with the person you like most and ending with the person you like least. Then justify your order of preference.

A plane crashed into a forest in Canada and the survivors landed on either side of a river. *L* was head over heels in love with *C*, and she wanted to get across the river to him. She couldn't swim so she asked *I* to make her a raft to cross on. But *I* was too busy trying to make a radio to send out an SOS message. She then asked *M* to help her, but he would only help her if she paid, and she had no money. When she asked *S*, he said, 'OK, but only if you sleep with me.'

S then built her a raft on which she crossed the river. When she told *C* what she had done to get across the river, he was furious and said he never wanted to see her again.

When *H* heard this he said, 'Then I'll marry you; I've always loved you.'

Self-portraits

Have a good look at your partner's drawing and answer these questions:

1 How old is this person?
2 Give him/her a nickname.
3 If this person was an animal, what animal would s/he be?
4 What kind of job would this person probably do?
5 Describe the sort of marriage partner this person might find.
6 Would this person make a good or bad parent? In what way?
7 What will s/he do when s/he retires?
8 How do you think s/he will die?

The statue game

Write as much as you want about each of the following:

1 You are walking along a path. You come to a statue. Where is the statue in relationship to the path?
2 What does the statue look like? Describe it in detail.
3 What can you see further along the path?
4 Say something to the statue.
5 Now you are the statue – say something back.
6 Tell the statue what changes you want *it* to make.
7 Now you are the statue again – tell the other person (your real self) how they need to change.

Jobs

From the list below choose those jobs which you'd most like to have. Give reasons. Then pick out the five jobs you would *least* like to have. Give reasons.

farm worker	plumber	dancer
bricklayer	postman/woman	author
bus driver	hairdresser	journalist
grocer	dock worker	computer operator
cook	pilot	psychiatrist
policeman/woman	clerk	time & motion person
air host/hostess	laboratory worker	social worker
carpenter	actor/actress	fireman/woman
miner	cleaner	dustman/woman
salesman/woman	waiter/waitress	large business owner
fisherman/woman	engineer	prostitute
gardener	factory worker	scientist
doctor (G.P.)	politician	manager
model	clergyman/woman	shop owner
musician	artist	child care officer
librarian	university teacher	paratrooper
nurse	draughtsman/woman	sailor
printer	architect	newsagent
house painter	telephonist	spy
electrician	secretary	research worker

The landscape game

Do a simple drawing in which you include the items listed below. Then describe your drawing.

Sun	Tree
Snake	Water
Path	Bushes
House	

Sharing a flat/ getting a job

Here are some personal advertisements. Read them carefully. Then write two advertisements, (a) proposing a flat-sharing arrangement, (b) asking for a job, for either yourself or a classmate.

Flat Sharing

MUSICIAN OFFERS large room to student (or two) in modern flat, N1. Low rent. Ring 278 6090 or messages: 604 2421.

TWO FEMALES (or couple) to share own bedroom in large house in SE25. £90 p.w. each, includes lounge, dining room, kitchen, bathroom, garden (583 9811 x 277 – Alan).

NOT CONSERVATIVE, LEFTISH. Professional couple, late twenties, needed to share spacious Surbiton flat with similar. £180 Close station. Phone 958 4600 pm.

N7 COUPLE wanted for double room in mixed house. £350 pcm each. Gardens, C/H, TV. Tel: 607 7134.

Jobs Wanted

GRAPHIC DESIGNER, writer, painter, decorator, singer, clerk, driver, humper, labourer, barman, etc. Returning soon, seeks interesting, well paid work. John Wevill, 128 Ledbury Road, Fishponds, Bristol, BS16 4AH.

GRADUATE, 24, speaks German, French, and Italian with experience in travel, industry and own car, seeks worthwhile employment. Tel: 01-385 8811 (evenings only).

HELP! Graduate, starting Cert-Ed October, seeks 'Community' work meanwhile. 690 1681.

I AM LOOKING for a varied job. Have car and enjoy driving. Vegetarian cooking. Looking after kids. Experience in buying and selling antiques. Can type. Knowledge of Russian. Box L896.

MALE Graduate, 22, seeks USEFUL employment. Fluent French. 761 2488.

BOOK-KEEPER Seeks part-time work evenings or weekends. For details please ring: 373 3621 after 6 pm.

CRAZY GUY, 23, model, bilingual. Wants work, Quebec/USA maybe. Box M229.

FINISH THE STORY

Writing practice.

The journalist

He heard the rumours that the government party had murdered half the people in the town. Pernamsuera, a little town half hidden in the jungle. It seems it had happened a week ago.

'A good story,' he thought. So he went there – it took 36 hours by train and canoe.

When he arrived he found the whole town asleep, not dead. It was siesta time, even the flies and the dogs were asleep. Nothing had happened in Pernamsuera at all.

He cabled his journalist friends and told them about this terrible massacre. 'Come at once – bring a TV crew and photographers.'

Two days later they arrived. He was fast asleep in a hammock under a banana tree.

Find-a-Love

Once upon a time, Find-a-Love, a computer dating organization, did a big advertising campaign. Diane and Terry were students and good friends – they filled out their forms at the same time. As they answered the questions, they discovered they were both looking for the same kind of man. Terry didn't take it very seriously as she was going out with a rather interesting guy at the time. His name was Joe. Diane, on the other hand, hadn't been out with anyone in months.

Several weeks later, Diane and Terry each received a list of five names from Find-a-Love. Diane was rather surprised to find Joe's name on her list. 'Aha,' she thought, 'So he sent in a form too.' She had heard a lot about Joe but she wasn't sure he knew about her. She wondered what to do.

Broken glass

'This bloke, he rang us on Christmas morning . . .'

'Christmas morning? Were you on duty then? Another pint?'

'Yeh, I'll have another, thanks. As I was saying, rang us on Christmas day. Said they'd broken into his shop and pinched a lot of jewellery . . .'

'A couple more, please, the same again.'

'Me and Joe were out on patrol – they called us up from the station, said the shop was on Exmoor Street, down by the market. Anyway, we shot down there as fast as we could, no traffic on Christmas morning. I had a good look at the window. It'd been broken, all right, but there was something very fishy about the way it'd been broken. Very strange. There was this small fat guy in the shop waiting for us. Then it hit me. I snapped the handcuffs on him and took him round to the station.'

'You nicked the shop-owner? Why?'

The piggy

Doctor Well, how are you today, Mr Thring?

Thring Not very well. Those pills didn't do any good at all. My stomach hurts and I feel dizzy when I stand up. Headaches too.

Doctor I'm sorry to hear that. Those pills are usually very good. Let's have a look at your tongue . . . Hmm, a nasty colour. Eyes pretty yellow, aren't they? Let's have a look at your chest now. Take a deep breath. Let it out now . . . slowly . . . slowly . . . Another. Mmmmm. All right, put your shirt on and let's take your blood pressure. Keep your arm relaxed – like this. Hmmm. All right, Mr Thring, you can roll your sleeve down. Now. What did you have to eat yesterday?

Thring Oh, a very light breakfast – cereal, egg, bacon, fried bread, sausages, toast, butter and coffee.

Doctor Hmm. And lunch?

Thring Let's see – soup, gnocchi, steak and kidney pie and apple pie with cream.

Doctor Cream?

Thring Well, apple pie's nothing without cream.

Doctor I see . . . never mind the rest. What about drink?

Thring Simple. A few sherries before lunch, beer with lunch and a few whiskies after lunch. Then a couple more whiskies between six and seven, a couple of sherries before dinner. And there was a wonderful wine with dinner. Very good indeed.

Doctor All right, that's enough, Mr Thring. Now I'm going to talk to you seriously. Of course those pills didn't help. If you take a hundred a day, they won't help. You're eating five times too much and drinking ten times too much for your condition. Your liver's bad, your stomach's even worse, your blood pressure's too high. You get dizzy, have headaches and you're tired all the time.

Thring Good God, doctor, that's exactly how I feel. How did you know?

Doctor It's my job to know. Now I'm going to . . .

The painter

A painter went to visit an old friend he had not seen for many years. They stayed up talking half the night. Just as they were going to turn in, the painter said, 'By the way, what happened to that old painting of mine?'

'Painting of yours? Mmmm, yes, I remember, the girl with the green scarf. I think it's up in the attic.'

'No, olive green background, and the scarf was very light mauve – you gave me £10 for it, d'you remember?'

The friend went up to the attic, brought the picture down, and propped it against the piano at the end of the room. 'Like a cup of tea?'

'Well, one more then.' The painter sat and stared at the painting while the other was out of the room making the tea.

'Y'know,' the painter said, getting up and going into the kitchen, 'I think that's one of my best bits of work – I want it back from you.'

'Christ,' the friend thought. 'The thing's worth £2000 with the reputation he's got now.' And then said out loud, 'Really?'

The book they took

They'd taken Mary's stones, worth more than £5000. The hi-fi equipment wasn't touched, but the radio was gone. They'd turned the whole place upside down but the only other thing they'd taken was the first chapter of his book!

He couldn't understand it. Thieves taking a chapter from a novel? He wanted to discuss it with Mary, but she lived in her own world. No point in bothering her.

He was glad he'd made a copy. At least he wouldn't have to re-write it.

About a week later, he got a strange phone call and soon after that a note. It was odd but he ignored it. Just happens sometimes, he thought to himself.

Three months passed and two hundred pages of the manuscript were done. He still had the last two chapters to write. He took the bundle of papers round to a publisher friend of his, who promised to read it over the weekend.

On Monday morning the phone rang. 'Listen, Ivan, the most terrible thing has happened – we were broken into last night . . . your book . . . well, it's vanished. The only bloody thing they took – your book!'

The President

Receptionist May I help you sir?
Man Ahh . . . yes.
Receptionist Whom do you wish to see?
Man Well, actually, ahh . . .
Receptionist I'll have to know who it is, sir.
Man Oh, well. It's really not important. I'll wait.
Receptionist I'm sorry, sir, but unless you tell me who you have an appointment with, I'm afraid I can't help you.

Man I'd . . . I'd like to see the President.
Receptionist The President!
Man Yes, the President. What's wrong with that?
Receptionist Have you got an appointment?
Man No. I don't need an appointment.
Receptionist But it's quite impossible, sir!
Man I'm an old friend.
Receptionist The President is an extremely busy person, sir. I'm terribly sorry.
Man Young woman, I demand that you contact the President and say I am here. I am sure the President would prefer that to the trouble I will cause . . . if you . . . this instant . . . don't get in touch with the President . . . and say I am here.

Shoes

'How long've these been here, then?'

'Nearly six months, I reckon, sir,' the warehouse man replied.

'Six months?' The customs inspector looked through his papers. 'Yes, they were unloaded last October. Yes, that's six months. No one's claimed them so we'll have to auction them.'

'Can't get over it, sir. 20,000 left-foot shoes . . .'

TEACHER'S NOTES

Contents

Teacher's Introduction

Challenge to Think provides a wide range of interesting problems for intermediate students who need to practise reading, writing, and especially oral skills, and revise and consolidate what they have already learned.

Students face the challenge of problem-solving situations, play popular thinking games and are invited to think creatively. The language becomes a means to an end: the students must grasp a problem through the language and reach a solution using the language. The teacher becomes a source of new language to help them to reach that goal.

Contents

The material is divided into sections which are grouped in three parts based on the language skills being practised:

Part 1 Speaking: seven sections of different types of spoken exercises.

Part 2 Reading and Speaking: eight sections of different types of exercises in which students read and then talk about a problem.

Part 3 Writing and Speaking: five sections of different types of exercises in which students write solutions to a problem and then share their work orally.

The main emphasis throughout is on spoken English.

This teacher's edition contains a clear step-by-step methodology, the solutions to the problems and keys to the exercises. Solutions are not provided where the exercises are open-ended

and 'answers' depend on students' perception of the problem. In this case, examples are provided.

The Student's book contains only the problems and exercises.

How to use this book

Challenge to Think is *not* designed to be used from cover to cover. The exercises should be used as follow-up and practice material up to several hours a week (with full-time students).

It is best to do one exercise from one of the sections and return to do another exercise from that section regularly, perhaps once every week or two. Over a period of time, the students will develop the skill required by that particular type of exercise and become aware of their own improvement.

Class time spent on the different exercises ranges from ten minutes in one section to sixty minutes in another. Because each section is so diverse, you can dip into this book as often as you like.

Most of the book is student-centred and involves students working together in pairs or small groups so that they can participate actively as much as possible. This frees the teacher from being the focus of the whole group's attention and allows him/her to spend the time going round and helping the students.

Some of the exercises in Parts 1 and 2 may be used for homework with a short introduction in the classroom. The reading stage of Part 2 and the writing stage of Part 3 can be done at home individually with the oral work done the next day in class.

PART 1 SPEAKING

Puzzle Stories

Aim   Practice in asking correct questions. Students are given an unexplained story. By asking a large number of questions, they eliminate wrong and irrelevant explanations of the story and find out what it is really about.

Class Time   10–15 minutes per story.

Methodology A   1 Get the class to read the story and ask you questions. You answer only 'yes', 'no', or 'not important'. For example, the procedure for the first story might be as follows:

Teacher	*(draws a picture on board of man with pack on back, explains 'pack', and 'field')* Look at story number 1 in your books and read it a few times. Now you're going to ask me as many questions as you can think of about each part of the story to find out how and why the man died.
Student	Died he because of the pack?
Teacher	Mmmmmm? *(incomprehension)*
Student	Did he dead because of the pack?
Teacher	Help him somebody.
Student	Did he die . . . .
Teacher	Yes, did he die because of the pack. Yes, he did.
Student	What was in the pack?
Teacher	I can't answer that. I can only answer 'yes' or 'no'.
Student	Was he very old?
Teacher	That's not important.
Student	There's a bomb in the pack.
Teacher	No, there isn't.

2 As in the above example, get students to correct each other's questions and do not answer unless the question is correct. Refuse to answer 'Wh' questions.

3 Make sure students are listening to each other's questions; otherwise they will waste a lot of time.

4 Accept all kinds of questions, e.g. interrogative questions, declarative questions, 'if' questions and statements, hypothetical statements; all of these are used by native speakers and should be encouraged.

5 Do not let students sit and think in silence. Direct their attention to parts of the story which they can ask about. Explain that by elimination of wrong information, they will find the solution.

6 If only a few students in the group are asking all the questions, give the class a clue. Accept no more questions. Get everyone to write down three questions and go round correcting them till everyone has got three. Then begin again, letting them use their questions and moving on from them.

7 When a student realizes the solution, make sure everyone understands it.

Methodology B

1 Divide the class into groups of six.

2 Take one person out of each group and tell them the story and solution where other students can't hear you. Make sure they understand it.

3 These students then act as question-masters as the teacher did in Methodology A. The teacher then goes round helping with language and listening in.

4 Use this method only after students have done several stories with you. It allows more student talking time. especially in a big group, but puts a lot of responsibility on students who are the question-masters.

Solutions

1 The man jumped from an aeroplane but his parachute didn't open.

2 She knows he is a liar.

3 The woman and the caller were both guests in a hotel, but didn't know each other. Their rooms were next to each other. The caller couldn't get to sleep because the woman was snoring.

4 It's daytime.

5 The two prisoners had been on horseback. The horses had their shoes on back to front, so the tracks in the snow seemed to be going from town Y to town X.

6 Two submarine officers see a destroyer through their periscope and want to dive.

7 Brought up since infancy by wolves, the two girls were recently found by humans and made to live indoors. They continue to behave the only way they know. (True story.)

8 The man had hiccups. The shock of having a gun pointed at him cured him.

9 The man brought a block of ice with him in a refrigerated lorry, put it in the hut and stood on it to hang himself. The ice melted and the water evaporated, leaving him dead and the hut empty.

10 The girl was a circus dwarf. Every night she measured her height against a piece of wood because she had a terrible fear she would grow. Another dwarf was jealous of her, because she was the star,

and sawed off the end of her piece of wood. She thought she had grown and so was heart-broken.

11   The man was blind and went to town B to see an eye-doctor, who restored his sight. When the train went into a tunnel on his return journey, the man thought he had gone blind again.

12   The couple are two goldfish whose bowl the dog has just knocked over.

13   These two little cannibals have eaten their father and mother and are now in an orphanage.

14   The man was blind. He went swimming every day and always left an alarm clock on shore to guide him back at the end of his swim. On this day, it was foggy. A ship sounded its fog bell. The man thought it was his alarm clock and swam towards the sound. The ship didn't see him because of the fog. It hit him and he drowned.

15   They will be boxing in a space satellite and so will be weightless. Hence they will be unable to knock each other down.

16   The woman was a Siamese twin whose attached twin would automatically have been involved, even though innocent. (This story usually provokes discussion about whether the judge would have to acquit a clearly guilty person.)

17   The couple will build their house on the South Pole.

18   The fishermen were out fishing in a shallow bay. An earthquake rolled the sea back, stranding their boats. Five minutes later, the sea roared back in a wall of water and they were all drowned. (True story, Chile 1960.)

19   The man was a fisherman and the black bag contained an enormous fish he had just caught. As he was telling his friend about the catch, he put his arms out to show the length of the fish. In the process, he smashed the glass on both sides of the phone booth.

20   This happened just after the outbreak of the Third World War. Bombs had dropped everywhere and this person was convinced he was the last living person in the world. He decided to commit suicide by jumping from the roof of a high building. Halfway down, he heard the phone ring inside the building and realized other people must be alive; hence the scream.

Three-Item Stories

Aim Practice in asking correct questions. The students are given three items. By asking a large number of questions about them, they can find out what the story is which links them.

Class Time 10–15 minutes per story.

Methodology 1 Get the class to think about the three items and explain any new language.

2 They ask you questions about them. You can answer only 'yes', 'no' or 'not important'.

3 Now read Methodology A and B in the section on Puzzle Stories (pages 84–5). You can do the three-item stories in exactly the same way.

Solutions 1 The accident was on a model railway.

2 A scientist in a town blockaded by enemy ships set one of the ships on fire by focussing the sun's rays on to it through a magnifying glass. The ship was made of wood and so burned.

3 A visitor to Amsterdam smuggled diamonds out of the country hidden in a teddy bear.

4 A concert pianist came to a concert prepared to play a Mozart concerto. When the orchestra started playing the opening bars, he realized in horror that they were playing a Beethoven concerto. He managed to readjust in time.

5 A boy was forced to spend his whole Saturday painting a long, high fence as a punishment. When his friends came to jeer at him he told them how much he *liked* doing it. They asked if they could have a go, too. In this way he got his friends to paint the whole fence for him.

6 Asked by a security man at the airport what he had in his many bags, the businessman said jokingly, 'A bomb, of course.' The other took him seriously and started a careful search of his luggage. The search delayed the plane's take-off and the businessman was fined for having deliberately caused the delay.

7 A driver drove a bride to her wedding in his bus. Twenty-two years before, her mother had given birth to her in a bus driven by the same driver.

8 The siege had dragged on for many weeks. Though his own people were near starvation the city commander knew that the attackers were tired of the siege. He took the town's last ox and had it tossed over the walls to give the impression that his people had plenty of food. The attackers lifted the siege.

9 A housewife, who wanted to make herself a dress, laid the pattern out on the carpet. She didn't notice that she was cutting round the pattern, through the material *and* through the carpet.

10 In an attempt to evade currency restrictions, a tourist·put bank notes in his shoes. At the airport there was a cloudburst and as he walked from the plane to the airport buildings he got wet feet. By the time he could remove his shoes there was very little left of the bank notes.

11 The owner of the valuable paintings had organized the theft in order to later claim the insurance money.

12 A man registered his car in his son's name and so avoided paying £500 in parking fines because, under British law, no one under ten can be prosecuted by the police.

Switch Sentences

Aim To get students to look closely at the meaning of a statement by contrasting it with a statement which contains the same words but in a different order. These exercises will provoke short intensive discussion and should be used mainly at higher intermediate level.

Class Time 30–40 minutes per group of four statements.

Methodology 1 Put the students in pairs.

2 Get them to look at the first statement and discuss what it means.

3 Then get them to switch two words in the sentence round and discuss the meaning of the new statement.
Example:
The women formed the club
The club formed the women.

4 When they understand the difference in meaning, get them to look at the specific examples of the meaning of the two statements listed after the first statement. They should classify them as belonging either to the original statement, the switched statement or both.

5 Then get them to look at the second statement in the group of four and discuss its meaning. Then they should switch two words round and discuss the meaning of the new statement. They can then talk about whether both statements are true or not, think of examples of each, etc.

6 When students have discussed all four statements and the switched statements, get the whole class to share what they have said and justify the classification they decided on in step 4 above.

Key 1 The women formed the club: examples a, b, c, g.
The club formed the women: examples a, b, d, e, f.

2 Schools are like prisons: examples a, b, c, d, e, f, g.
Prisons are like schools: examples a, b, c, d, e, f, g, h.

3 People cause accidents: examples b, c, d, f, g, h.
Accidents cause people: examples a, c, d, e, g.

4 All children become adults: examples a, b, c, d, e, f, g.
All adults become children: examples a, b, d, e, g, h.

5 Industry determined the landscape: examples a, b, c, e, f, g.
The landscape determined industry: examples a, d, e.

6 To live to eat: examples a, b, c, e.
To eat to live: examples d, f, g, h.

7 When wages rise they inflate prices: examples a, b, e, f, g, h
When prices rise they inflate wages: examples a, b, c, d, f, h

8 Unemployment causes poverty: examples a, b, e, g, h
Poverty causes unemployment: examples a, c, d, f, h

9 Animals are our friends: examples a, c, e, h
Our friends are animals: examples b, d, f, g

Switch Photos

Aim To provoke intensive discussion of the links between the subjects of two photographs. Language used will include description, conditional statements, and cause and effect. Use mainly at higher intermediate level.

Class Time 15–20 minutes per pair of photographs.

Methodology 1 Put the students in pairs.

2 Ask them to look at the two photographs as if they were a sentence: Photograph A, therefore Photograph B.

3 Get them to explain and discuss the meaning of this 'picture sentence'.

4 Then get them to make a new 'picture sentence' by switching the two photographs so that: Photograph B, therefore Photograph A.

5 Ask them to discuss the new causal relationship and other relationships between the two pictures.

6 Get the whole class together to share what they have said in pairs and compare their conclusions.

To use the single photograph on page 16:

7 Ask each student to make his or her own drawing of what follows from the photograph.

8 Ask the students to get up and mill around the classroom, cocktail party style. They should explain how the photograph relates to their drawings to as many people as possible in the group.

Causes and Consequences

Aim To get students to discuss all the possible causes and consequences of a factual statement.

Class Time 25 minutes per group of three statements.

Methodology 1 Put the students into groups of four.

2 Ask them to look at the three statements in the group. Tell them that these are statements of fact. (They should not discuss whether the statements are true or not, but take them as given.)

3 Get them to think of as many causes and consequences of each fact as they can. They should spend no more than five minutes per statement.

Example Doctors in rich countries advise people to stay slim.

Causes: Rich countries grow more than enough food.
People can afford to buy as much to eat as they want.
People eat too much.
People eat too much fattening food.
Overweight is causing other illnesses, e.g. heart attacks, etc.

Consequences: People ignore the advice and have to see the doctor more often or go to hospital or even die.
People go on diets, do more exercise, etc.
Food manufacturers produce non-fattening foods, etc.

Designs

Aim To provoke discussion and criticism of the designs of everyday objects by considering imaginary designs or alternatives to existing ones. Students then create their own alternative designs, and describe them.

Class Time 30–40 minutes per design.

Methodology 1 Put the students in groups of four.

2 Get them to look at the questions and discuss the designs, using

personal experience, what they have seen in advertisements or while travelling, and what they know of other countries.

3 You go round helping them with new language.

4 When they have answered all the questions, get them to draw their own designs, either as a group with a group artist, or individually. If you have enough board space in the room, get them to draw their designs on the board.

5 Encourage them to ignore reality and let their imaginations go. These exercises can be a great deal of fun if students feel free to create.

6 Get each group or individual to explain their design to the rest of the class.

Examples of designs which students have invented are:

The Bath: TV built into wall with handy controls, sponge on bottom of bath for comfort, etc.

The Traffic Jam Car: car with wings, car with helicopter top, car with book library, etc.

The TV Phone: background music, wigs to put on, changeable background scenes, wardrobe, etc.

Context and Meaning

Aim To show students how a simple statement can have a variety of meanings depending on the context in which it is said. In some cases, a change of intonation is also appropriate in a specific context and can also be looked at.

Class Time 30 minutes per exercise.
30 minutes extra with follow-up exercise.

Methodology 1 The first time you do these exercises, go over the example with the class. Explain the purpose of the exercise.

2 Put students in pairs (or groups of up to four with a large class).

3 In part (a) of the exercise, they are given a statement and five situations in which it might be said. They should decide what the statement actually means in each situation.

4 In part (b) of the exercise, they are given a statement and what it might mean in some context. They should think up a situation in which the statement would have that meaning.

5 In part (c) students should think up different situations in which the given statement would have different meanings and what these would be.

6 There may be more than one context possible for each meaning and vice versa. There is no one correct answer.

7 Students may note down their answers as in the example. You should go round helping them.

8 When they have finished all three parts, get each pair or group to tell the class their answers. Check that the meanings they give are actually implied by the context and vice versa, especially in part (c).

Follow-Up Exercise   Put students in pairs. Give each pair one of the contexts in the exercise and get them to prepare a short role-play which contains the original statements and illustrates its implied meaning in that context. Give them five minutes to prepare it and let them act it out for the class.

PART 2 READING AND SPEAKING

Two-in-One Stories

Aim   An intensive reading exercise. The lines of two stories are mixed together out of sequence. Students must separate and sequence the stories. They then tell each other the stories from memory.

Class Time   20–30 minutes per pair of stories.

Methodology

1 Tell the students they are going to find two stories mixed together and out of sequence.

2 Working individually, they should separate the two stories and put the lines in the correct order. They should use the numbers of the sentences rather than copying them out.

3 Go round helping them as needed.

4 When most of them have finished, ask them to read the lines out in the correct order for each story. Go round the class, asking each student to read one line to do this. Give time for corrections and questions.

5 If a number of students have found it difficult, go over the clues in each story which indicate the sequence.

6 Put the students in pairs. Tell them to look at the two stories quietly for a minute and fix them firmly in their minds.

7 Get them to close their books. Each student should tell his/her partner one of the stories with the other student correcting any mistakes.

Solutions   The Stork: 1, 4, 10, 8, 6, 2.
The Company Chairman: 5, 3, 9, 7.

The Farmer: 7, 1, 6, 4, 8.
The Invitation: 3, 5, 2, 9.

A Stranger in London: 14, 6, 15, 12, 1, 13, 9, 5, 3.
The New Hedge Clipper: 8, 2, 11, 4, 10, 7.

The Railway Ticket: 4, 1, 7, 13, 9, 6, 12.
Aesop's Fable: 3, 8, 10, 14, 2, 11, 5, 15.

The Loan: 9, 4, 1, 3, 6, 11.
The Burglar: 2, 8, 5, 10, 7.

The General's Visit: 6, 9, 7, 1, 4.
No Teeth: 3, 5, 2, 8.

Contradictions

Aim   Quick intensive reading practice. Students read a short passage containing a series of contradictions and react to them. Language of agreement and disagreement.

Class Time   10 minutes per story.

Methodology   1 Get the students to read only **one** sentence at a time, no more.

2 In either the first or second sentence, they will begin finding contradictory elements. Don't tell them this – let them react on their own. When they see something odd, they may react as follows:

That's a misprint.
That's impossible because . . . .
If *X* is true, *Y* can't be true.

Let them toss these ideas around and have fun with them.

This is how one group reacted to the first sentence of Exercise 1:
John Brown is a butcher who always sells good stale bread.

Student 1   There's something wrong with this.
Student 2   Butchers don't sell bread.
Student 3   Yes, and if the bread is stale it can't be good.
Student 4   In a grocer's shop you could buy meat *and* bread.
Student 1   A butcher might want to buy bread but he wouldn't be selling it.
Student 5   Buy it? What for?
Student 3   To put in sausages . . .

3 Get them to read the next sentence only, and react to this. They may refer backwards to previous items, but stop them referring forwards.

4 Carry on one sentence at a time. The effect of the contradictions piling up will bring more and more students to react and disagree with one another.

5 The point of this exercise is not the correction of the contradictions, but the discussion they provoke. It is most effective if you say nothing except when they should go on to the next sentence.

6 You might also try putting these exercises on tape with long pauses between each sentence. You could then play an exercise one sentence at a time, stopping for comments but saying nothing.

Matchings

Aim   For discussion of the meaning of newspaper headlines and captions, and speculation about what the accompanying articles or cartoons are about. Followed by fast reading of the actual articles to match them to the headlines.

Class Time   20–30 minutes per group of headlines and articles.

Methodology
1 Put the students into pairs.

2 Tell them to look at the headlines. (In the first group, the headlines are printed in the top half of the page, with the articles underneath; in succeeding groups, the headlines are on the left-hand page and the articles on the right-hand page.)

3 Explain any new vocabulary and then ask them to choose four or five headlines and discuss what the accompanying articles might be about. They should try and think of several possibilities. Go round helping them and stop them after about five minutes.

4 Now get them to look at the articles and match all the headlines to their corresponding articles individually. They should not read every article in detail as this is a fast reading exercise.

5 Put the correct key up on the board or get students to read out their answers.

6 You might then look at one or more articles in depth, particularly any they had difficulty matching up.

Key
Page 35:   1e, 2c, 3b, 4d, 5a.   •

Pages 36–7:   1e, 2c, 3f, 4d, 5h, 6i, 7j, 8b, 9a, 10g.

Pages 38–9:   1i, 2c, 3a, 4d, 5h, 6b, 7j, 8e, 9g, 10f.

Pages 40–1:   1b, 2i, 3j, 4a, 5f, 6d, 7h, 8c, 9g, 10e.

Pages 42–3:   1b, 2c, 3i, 4h, 5d, 6g, 7j, 8e, 9a, 10f.

Deduction Puzzles

Aim
Intensive reading practice and oral practice of a range of conditionals and deductive language. Students read a story which poses a problem and answer questions which lead to the solution.

Class Time
20–30 minutes per puzzle.

Methodology

1 Get students to read the story only and explain any new language.

2 Get them to read the story a second time.

3 Put them in pairs.

4 Tell them to work through the questions, jotting down the answers. They must answer the questions in order as one leads on from the last one. If they answer all questions correctly, they will have found the solution to the puzzle.

5 If some students finish faster than others, get them to help the slower students.

6 Then go over the answers by firing the questions orally round the class. If anyone doesn't understand an answer, get another student to explain it.

Solutions

The Parachutes

1 They would've caught him if he'd stayed on the plane because they would have been waiting at the airport.

2 He had a chance of escaping by parachute because they weren't expecting him to.

3 He didn't have a better chance with a hostage.

4 Because the police had become good at catching people who had hostages with them.

5 I'd have thought he wanted me to jump with him.

6 I'd have been sure to give him good parachutes.

7 Otherwise I might have got a bad one and been killed jumping with him.

The Lawyers

A Alfred's point of view:

1 (b) Alfred's lost the case if the judge says he must pay.

2 (b) But if Alfred loses the case, he needn't pay Bertram, according to his agreement with Bertram.

3 (a) Alfred's won the case if the judge says he needn't pay.

4 (b) If the judge says he needn't pay, then he needn't pay, according to the law.

B Bertram's point of view:

1 (a) Bertram's won the case if the judge says Alfred must pay him.

2 (a) If the judge says he must pay, then he must, according to the law.

3 (b) Bertram's lost the case if the judge says Alfred needn't pay him.

4 (a) But if Alfred wins the case, then he must pay Bertram according to their agreement.

C This doesn't sound right at all. Neither of them is right. Both of them accent the terms of their private agreement when it suits them and the law when it suits them. But their agreement and the law contradict each other in this situation.

The Four Babies

1 Only one of the babies is a boy, Bernard.

2 The nurse should have known which baby Bernard was because he's the only boy.

3 No, his hair hasn't started to grow yet.

4 You know that Diana is the baby who has a lot of hair because the first clue says it wasn't Anna or Carmen and the third clue says it wasn't Bernard. The sixth clue says her hair colour is red.

5 The nurse knows that Diana kicks a lot.

6 Anna can't be the baby who cries a lot because happy babies don't cry a lot.

7 That means Carmen is the only baby left who could be the cry-baby.

8 The nurse also remembers that she has a birthmark by her right ear.

9 That leaves only Anna who is the fattest baby.

10 Anna is the fattest and is very happy; Bernard sucks his thumb quietly and has no hair; Carmen is a cry-baby and has a birthmark by her right ear; Diana has a lot of red hair and kicks a lot.

The Shipwrecked Man

1 (a) If the first man is the shipwrecked man, he must have told the truth and said he was.

2 (a) If the first man is not the shipwrecked man, he must have lied and said he was.

3 (c) No, we can't tell if the first man is lying or not because he must answer yes in either case.

4 (c) If the first man says yes in either case, then the second man is truthfully reporting what he said. If the second man had been a liar, he would have had to say no.

5 (a) Only one of the men can be telling the truth.

6 (c) Since the second man is telling the truth, the first man must be lying.

7 (b) The second man is the real shipwrecked man.

8 (c) The third man is in the story because he would have been the shipwrecked man if the other two had been lying.

The Murderers

1 Five men were arrested.

2 All five of them deny killing Foxy.

3 Four of them must be telling the truth when they say they are innocent.

4 Four of them accuse one of the others of the murder – Daddy Long Legs, Fatty, Square-Head and Big-Nose.

5 Shorty doesn't accuse another man of the killing.

6 He says that the others say they are all innocent.

7 Yes, the others all do say they are innocent.

8 Yes, that means Shorty's second statement is true.

9 Shorty says that he too is innocent.

10 No, his first *and* second statements cannot both be true.

11 Then his first statement must be false.

12 So Shorty is guilty because he is lying when he says he's innocent.

The Scientists and the Watches

1 The two scientists were arguing about whose watch was better.

2 They couldn't continue the experiment because there was something wrong with both watches.

3 They observed the watches for a couple of hours without speaking.

4 They realized the Swiss watch was losing sixty minutes an hour.

5 (b) If a watch is losing sixty minutes in sixty minutes, it's stopped.

6 (a) Once in every twelve hours the Swiss watch would show the right time.

7 The Japanese watch was losing 120 minutes every sixty minutes.

8 (c) It is going backwards if it loses 120 minutes every sixty minutes. In other words, every time a clock telling the correct time moved forward an hour, the Japanese clock moved back exactly an hour.

9 The Japanese watch will show the correct time *twice* in every 12-hour period, i.e. every six hours.

10 The scientist with the Japanese watch was right when he said, 'My watch is right more often than yours.'

11 Discuss the absurdity of the entire argument. Neither watch *tells* the correct time – they only *show* it. You wouldn't know they were showing it without a third watch to refer to.

The Sultan and the Cheat

1 There were ten goldsmiths.

2 Only one of them was a cheat.

3 Each coin the cheat made was one gram short.

4 (b) The sultan found the cheat by weighing coins.

5 He weighed the coins he took from them once only.

6 (c) He took the coins to weigh from all of the goldsmiths.

7 If he'd taken all 100 coins and weighed them together, they'd have been ten grams short.

8 Yes, he would have known that one of the smiths had cheated.

9 No, he wouldn't have known which smith had cheated because all 100 would have been on the scales together.

10 He would take three from the third, four from the fourth, five from the fifth, etc. up to ten from the tenth.

11 That would be 55 coins altogether.

12 (b) If nobody had cheated, the total weight of those 55 coins should have been 550 grams.

13 The coins he weighed were 540 grams.

14 So ten of the coins he weighed were made by the cheat.

15 The tenth goldsmith was the cheat.

The Prisoners

1 X could see the two poles that Y and Z were tied to.

2 He saw that Y's pole was black and Z's pole was white.

3 If X had seen two black poles instead, he would have known that the remaining three poles, including his own, were white.

4 As it was, X had to say he didn't know, because his pole could have been black or white.

5 Y realizes that X had seen either two white poles or else one black and one white pole.

6 Y could see Z's pole, which was white.

7 Y couldn't tell the colour of his pole.

8 He had to say he didn't know.

9 Z knew that, at most, only one of the two poles (his and Y's) could be black.

10 He also knew this: if Y had seen Z's pole was black, Y would have known his own pole was white.

11 Yes, he knew that his own pole had to be white and he was able to tell the king.

12 The three prisoners were freed, as the king had promised.

Four Women

1 The women were told to stand up only if they saw more black than white marks.

2 All four women stood up.

3 So all four of them saw more black than white marks.

4 If the wise woman had made three white marks and one black, none of them would have stood up.

5 If she'd made two white and two black marks, the two women with white marks would've stood up.

6 If she'd made one white and three black marks, all four of them would've stood up.

7 If she'd made four black marks, all four women would've stood.

8 Either of two colour combinations could be the right one – three black/one white or four black.

9 All four women would have realized this, assuming they were good thinkers.

10 If one of the marks was white, the three women with black marks would've seen it.

11 They then would've known their own marks were black, since at least three had to be black.

12 All three of them would have said this immediately.

13 But no one said anything for what seemed a long time.

14 So none of them could have seen a white mark.

15 The woman who finally spoke up realized first that all four marks were black and said that all four marks were black, including hers.

Follow-up   1 They all had an equal chance because they all saw the same thing on the others' foreheads. Thus, each of them had the same information to work from.

2 The one with a white mark wouldn't have had an equal chance because she'd have had different information from the others. The others would've seen her white mark and immediately known they had black marks; she wouldn't know about her own mark till they had spoken.

3 Four white marks would also make it fair. No one would stand up and there would then be the choice between three white/one black and four white.

4 The answer to this question is open to discussion.

5 This answer is also open.

Psychology Questionnaires

Aim   For discussion of how students have felt or acted in a variety of situations or how they would feel. Followed by role-play of some of the situations. Each questionnaire is about a particular emotion.

Class Time   50–60 minutes per questionnaire.

Methodology   1 Give pieces of chalk (or board pens) to as many students as fit round the board and ask them to come to the board. Get them to draw whatever comes into their heads on the subject of the questionnaire, e.g. laughter. As they finish get more students up so that they quickly fill the board with drawings. Keep them moving quickly.

2 Ask each student to explain their drawings.

3 Put the students into groups of four.

4 Get them to go through the questionnaire, asking each other the questions and talking about what they have done in situations which interest them to discuss. Give them a time limit for this, about twenty minutes. It is not important if they do not do every question.

5 Then get the students in pairs.

6 Ask each pair to pick one situation from the questionnaire and invent a role-play that illustrates it. These should be brief.

7 Get some or all of the pairs to act out their role-plays.

Role-Play the News

Aim   Students read a newspaper article, create a role-play from it and act it out. This exercise should be used at higher intermediate level.

Class Time   50–60 minutes per article.

Methodology

1 Get the students to read one of the articles silently and explain any new language.

2 Put them into groups of three or four.

3 Get them to think of different ways they could act out the story and choose one. They can add or leave out any characters they like. They can also choose to act out something which occurred before or after the actual story in the article.

4 Give them about fifteen minutes to discuss and rehearse their role-plays. Go round helping with language.

5 Get each group to act theirs out in front of the class. You take notes on the language used, particularly expressions they might have used which they didn't know and point these out briefly after each group has finished.

Example   Here are some possible role-plays students might do for the article 'Publican jailed for assault':

1 the argument between the tax man and publican as the furniture was being removed from the pub.

2 the conversation between Mr and Mrs S— after the tax man had left the pub with the furniture.

3 a lawyer questioning the tax man in court.

4 the conversation between Mr and Mrs S— when the tax bill arrived and they decided not to pay it.

Lies, All Lies!
Spot the lies!

Aim   Students analyse short reading passages to find the lies in them.

Class Time   40–50 minutes.

Methodology

1 Put students in groups of four or in pairs.

2 Tell them to read the first passage and look at the illustration. They should then look for lies in the passage, usually more than

one. Where there are illustrations, some or all of the lies are linked to them.

3 When they think they have found all the lies, they should go on to the next passage.

4 You go round helping with new language in the passages and giving clues if they are finding it difficult to locate the lies.

5 When they have analysed all eight passages, get the whole class together and ask different students to name one lie they found in a passage. Get them to correct each other's mistakes if possible and tell them any lies that they missed out.

6 If you prefer, do only four of the passages in one lesson and go back to do the other four another day.

Key

Come South!	Almost no one lives in the shaded areas of the map, which is a vast desert. Those who do are very poor.
'No time to go to school'	The 90 days the girl subtracts for summer holidays in reality include 90 nights, but she has already subtracted the nights. In other words she is counting the same things twice or more.
Keep off the roads!	There were hardly any cars on the roads thirty years ago compared with today.
Union wants 50% increase in wages	50% of ½ is a ¼. If this union leader is successful, his men will get 75% of what they were getting last year. They will not regain all they lost.
Cheaper and cheaper!	There are no figures on the vertical axis of the graph, so the prices may have fallen steeply by 0.008 of a penny.
Bungalows for sale	The average may be 28 degrees but this does not stop day temperatures being over 40 and night ones sub-zero.
Crime wave	The fact that the papers report more crimes does not mean more crimes are being committed.
Join up!	The army is mainly made up of young healthy people. The population of London includes invalids and old people.

What is it?

Aim	To guess what something is from a deceptive description of it.
Class Time	15–20 minutes.
Methodology	1 Put the students in groups of four or in pairs.
	2 Tell them they have to read the description of the object or thing and guess what it is.

3 Go round helping with language and give them clues if they are stuck.

4 Get the whole class together and check that they have all guessed right. Look at the descriptions with them and get them to point out the clues that give away the answer.

Key

Cut price central heating	Breakfast cereal.
For Sale	Camel.
House Agent's Advertisement	Houseboat *or* caravan.
For Sale	Coffin.

What is a lie?

Aim Students talk about short situations in which someone does not tell the truth.

Class Time 20 minutes.

Methodology 1 Put the students in groups of four.

2 Get them to read the first situation and discuss the questions that follow it. They should do this for the six situations.

Questionnaire: When do you lie?

Aim Group discussion.

Class Time 20 minutes.

Methodology 1 Put the students in groups of four.

2 Get them to answer the questionnaire individually.

3 Students compare and discuss their answers within the group.

4 Get them to count how many a's, b's or c's they answered and read them the key: 'If you answered mainly a's, you are a stupid truth-teller; if you answered mainly b's, you are a reasonable liar; if you answered mainly c's, you have a good imagination and realize this is a bad questionnaire.'

Moral Issues

Aim Intensive reading of a passage that raises moral issues for debate.

Class Time 20–30 minutes per passage.

Methodology 1 Pre-teach any new language from the passage.

2 Put students into groups of four.

3 Ask them to read through the passage and then discuss the problems and issues raised in the questions or points following the passage. (Passage 2, *In court*, needs no discussion points.)

4 Halfway through the discussion, get one student from each group to move to another group and give a report. They then continue the discussion.

5 When they have finished, ask the class if they would like to hear what conclusions the other groups reached. If they would, get each group to give a brief report.

PART 3 WRITING AND SPEAKING

Creative Drills

Aim Students are given an unusual problem and must think up as many solutions to it as they can. They write down the solutions using suggested structures. They then criticize each other's solutions. Structures include: suggestions, advice, conditionals, verb tenses, conjunctions, relative clauses and descriptions.

Class Time 20–30 minutes per problem.

Methodology
1 Get students to work individually or in pairs.

2 Tell them to read through the problem and note down as many solutions as they can think of, using the structures given. Tell them solutions can be funny, crazy, impossible or realistic. Do *not* start them off with examples; let them work with no help on ideas at all.

3 Go round giving help with vocabulary, etc. If you see that a student isn't getting any ideas on his/her own, suggest one or two possible ones.

4 Encourage students to use all the suggested structures more than once but accept other correct statements as well.

5 When a number of students have finished, get the whole class together and go round the class asking students to read out their favourite solutions. This may generate critical comments – encourage this.

6 When students have given a fair number of solutions, you might ask questions like:

Which solution is the craziest? Most dangerous?
Which solution won't work? Cost the most?
Which would women do? Men?

and so on to fit the topic.

Example of Students' Solutions
Problem 1: How to show someone you are angry without saying anything.

Possible Solutions: By throwing something at them.
You can make it clear by slamming the door in their face.
You can let them know by refusing to speak to them.
By stepping hard on their foot under the table.
You can show them by hanging up the phone on them.

By talking to someone they are jealous of.
You can show them by sulking.
By being tensely polite to them.
You can make it clear by reading a paper in front of them.

Problem 2:   My kitchen is swarming with flies! How can I get rid of them?

Possible Solutions: How about spraying the kitchen with fly spray?
What about closing the window?
One way'd be to move to another house.
I'd mix some poison with sugar and put it out.
How about cleaning the kitchen up?
What about getting a tame swallow?
One way'd be to have a basin full of trout.
I'd get a fly-swat.
What about hanging up a sticky paper?
How about fumigating the place?

Creative Crosswords

Aim   Writing, leading to discussion.

Class Time   20 minutes per crossword, probably more for crossword 4.

Methodology

Crosswords 1–2   1 In these two exercises, students are given a completed crossword puzzle and must write the clues, which are definitions. (Human relationships in 1 and familiar places and things in 2.)

2 When they have finished writing the clues, get them to read out what they have written to the class, as they are likely to have different definitions.

Crossword 3   1 In this exercise, students must fill in the crossword puzzle. They are practising the structure (*have something done*) by reading and re-reading the clues.

2 When they have finished, check that their answers are correct.

Key   *Across*   1 porter   3 nobody   6 barber

Down   1 printer   2 scabs   4 yeti   5 vet

Crossword 4   1 Students compose a grid and fill it in with a name of their own choosing. They then write the clues.

2 Compare different grids, names and clues and discuss which are the most successful.

Key   Here is a simple grid and clues for people who have things done to them.

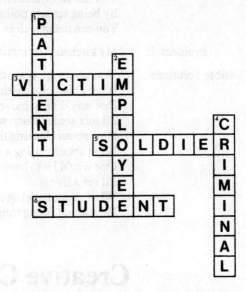

1 One who is given medical treatment.   2 One who is made to work.   3 One who is killed.   4 One who is sent to prison.   5 One who takes orders in an army.   6 One who is taught.

Here is a grid and clues for people who do things to others.

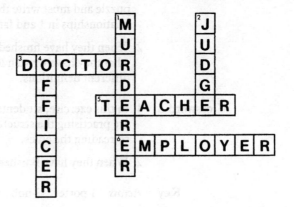

1   One who kills another.   2 One who sends another to prison. 3 One who gives medical treatment.   4 One who gives orders in an army.   5 One who teaches another.   6 One who makes another work.

What's in a Blot?

Aim   Writing, leading to discussion.

Class Time   20 minutes per blot.

Methodology   1 Students look at the ink blots and write down what they see in them, using the structures.

2 When they have finished, get them to read out their answers and criticize each other's.

3 You can use this section four different times, using a different ink blot and only some of the structures each time.

Describe Yourself

Aim   This section has seven different exercises, including writing descriptions of people, places or things and analysing what their descriptions mean, doing a simple drawing and analysing it, listing preferences from a drawing or a list and talking about why they are preferences. Each of these exercises is based on popular psychology games which are played socially, used in job interviews, etc.

Class Time   20–30 minutes per exercise.

Methodology 1
The Path Game   1 Get students to read the questions and explain any new language.

2 Get them to write brief answers to each of the questions. Tell them they can write whatever they like. Do *not* give them examples of any kind. Go round correcting and helping with new language.

3 When they have finished, ask all (or some) of them to read out what they wrote for No. 1. Then explain the symbolic meaning, using the key below. Do the same for each question, explaining the meaning after they have read out their answers.

Key   1 How they see life.

2 Their attitude to small problems.

3 Their attitude to big problems.

4 Their attitude to the opposite sex.

5 Their political tendencies.

6 What they think death is like.

7 What they think is after death.

Methodology 2
The Survivors

1 Get students to read the passage and make a list of all the people in the story, starting with the person they like the most and working down to the person they like least.

2 When they have finished, ask some (or all) of them to put their lists up on the board and justify their own preferences.

3 Then read them the key and let them react.

Key   L = love
       I = integrity
       M = money
       S = sex
       C = convention
       H = home

Methodology 3
Self-portraits

1 Ask students to draw pictures of themselves, emphasizing the features they think most important. They should not look at each other's pictures or put names on them.

2 You take the pictures, shuffle them and hand one out to each student, face down.

3 Now get them to answer the questions about the pictures they have in the student's book.

4 Get each student to read out what he/she has written about their picture and other students should try to guess whose self-portrait the picture is.

Methodology 4
The Statue Game

1 Get students to answer the questions and write the dialogue as directed in the student's book.

2 Ask students to read out what they have written for No. 1, then for each of the other questions.

3 Put the students into groups of four.

4 Get them to discuss, referring to what they have written:
a) the symbolic meanings of the statue, the path, the area around the statue, and the dialogue between the 'self' and the statue.
b) what this game tells them about themselves.

Methodology 5
Jobs

1 Ask the students to make a list of those jobs they would most like to do and the five jobs they would least like to do from the list in their books.

2 Put the students in groups of four.

3 Each student reads out his/her lists to the group and explains why he/she would or wouldn't like to do them. The group then discusses what the lists reveal about the person who wrote them.

Methodology 6
The Landscape Game

1 Ask the students to do a simple drawing, including all the items listed in their books.

2 Put them in pairs or small groups to look at each other's drawings.

3 Give them the key and get them to discuss and compare their drawings in light of it.

Key

sun = religion
snake = sexuality
path = ambition
house = self
tree = attitude to father
water = attitude to mother
bushes = friends

Methodology 7
Sharing a Flat/Getting a Job

1 Do this exercise only after students know each other a bit.

2 Get all the students to write their names on a bit of paper. Take the pieces, shuffle them and hand one out to each student at random.

3 Get them to read the personal advertisements in their books carefully and explain any new language. They should use these examples as models for what they are going to write.

4 They should then imagine that they are the person whose name they have been given. They should write two advertisements as that person, one proposing a flat-sharing arrangement and the other asking for work. You go round helping with language.

5 When they have finished, get each student to read out what they have written. The class has to guess who each student has written the advertisements for.

Finish the Story

Aim   Students write the end of an unfinished story, using either narrative or dialogue and then look at each other's endings.

Class Time   30–45 minutes per story.

Methodology

1 Get students to read the story and explain any new language.

2 Put students in pairs. Working in pairs means they will be able to plan and talk about what they are writing, and students who are stronger in spoken English can get the benefit of working with someone whose writing is better. One of the two can do the writing down as they work.

3 Get them to write endings to the story, either using dialogue, narrative or both. Give them a time limit, 20–30 minutes.

4 You go round correcting their papers as much as possible, helping with new language.

5 When they have finished, you can either:
   a) Choose several of the better endings and read them out (with the authors if they are in dialogue form);
   b) Get the students to read their own endings out to the class, making sure everyone understands them;
   c) Get them to circulate their endings round the room so that they can read each other's endings.

6 Reading or listening to other endings provides most of the pleasure of this exercise as students enjoy seeing what others have done differently from themselves.